TABLE (

CHAPTER ONE
INTRODUCTION TO PROPERTY MANAGEMENT

The importance of the skill-set and know how of property monitoring and management cannot be overemphasized especially for professionals and career personnel in the field.

Property management is the process, control, maintenance and oversight of real estate and physical property. This can include real estate properties, residential, industrial, and property. Management shows the need for immovable property to be cared for and controlled, with due consideration for its useful life and condition. This is quite similar to managerial position in any company.

Property is a term that describes anything that has legal title over a person or a business, affording owners certain enforceable rights over those items. Examples of property that may be tangible or intangible include automotive vehicles, industrial equipment, furniture, and real estate-the last of which is often referred to as "real property." Most properties hold current or potential monetary value and are therefore considered to be assets. But, in some cases, assets may be liabilities at the same time. Case in point: if a person sustains an injury to the property of a corporation, the business owner may be legally liable for paying the medical bills of the injured party. To further explain the concept of property, let's look to understand some key factors;

- Property is any object which has legal title to a individual or company.
- Land can be tangible objects, such as buildings, cars or equipment, or it can refer to intangible things that hold the promise of future value, such as stock and bond certificates.
- Intellectual property refers to inventions such as patent and logo designs.
- -Land owners may also have liabilities, as is the case if a business owner is on the hook for medical bills resulting from a client incurring injury on the grounds of his company.

Proceeding on the subject matter, we will further breakdown the topic for a better understanding of what we are talking about. Now let us explain what management means.

Management (or management) is an entity's administration, whether it is a corporation, a non-profit agency or a government body. Management requires activities to develop an organization's agenda and organize the actions of its employees (or volunteers) to achieve their goals through the use of available resources, such as financial, environmental, technical, and human capital. The word "management" may also apply to those individuals who run an organization. Further more, Management includes determining the task, purpose, processes, rules and manipulation of an organization's human resources to contribute to the company's success. This implies efficient communication: an organizational environment (as opposed to a physical or mechanical mechanism) implies human motivation and implies some form of positive progress or program result. In an individual's viewpoint, management does not need to be viewed exclusively from an organizational point of view, as management is an important role [quantify] in enhancing one's life and relationships. Management is also everywhere and it has a broader variety of applications. Based on this, management must have humans.

Property management is also the management of personal property, equipment, tooling, and physical capital assets obtained and used to create, repair, and maintain deliverables of end goods. Property management involves the processes, procedures, and manpower needed to manage the life cycle of all acquired property as described above, including acquisition, control, accountability, liability, repair, usage, and disposal. Property management can also be said to be the oversight of residential, commercial and/or industrial property, including apartments, detached homes, condominium units, and shopping centers. It usually includes handling property owned by another party or organization. On behalf of the owner, the property manager acts to preserve the value of the property while generating revenue.

A single-family house, condominium, or multi-family building owner may engage a skilled property management company in the services. The company must then advertise the rental property, manage inquiries from tenants, screen applicants, pick appropriate candidates, draw up a lease agreement, make an inspection transfer, transfer the tenant(s) into the property and receive rental income. The company would then manage any maintenance concerns, provide financial statements to the owner(s) and any other information concerning the land.

A property manager is an person or organization that is hired to supervise a real estate unit's day-to-day operation. Land owners and real estate developers usually employ property managers when the assets themselves are reluctant or unable to be managed. The cost of hiring a property manager is tax-deductible against the property 's revenue generated. Complex homes, shopping centers, and business offices are growing forms of commercial property managed by property managers.

Property managers provide an perfect solution for investors who do not live in close proximity to their rental properties or simply do not like dealing with tenants, toilets etc. There are several real estate investors, especially institutional real estate investors, who do not wish to be hands-on with the investment.

The duties of the property manager may include managing and organizing building repairs and work orders, performing light handy and cleaning work, addressing tenant issues and grievances, advertisement, showing and leasing empty apartments, collecting and depositing rent, and periodically interacting with the property owner about the property's status. The property manager is the owner's eyes and ears on the property making sure problems are dealt with quickly and the property itself is properly cared for.

Real estate is a property consisting of land and buildings thereon, together with its natural resources such as crops, minerals or water; immovable property of this nature; an interest in this (also) real estate, (more generally) buildings or housing in general.

Residential property can contain either a single-family structure or a multi-family structure that is available for occupation or non-business. Residences can be classified by neighboring residences and land, and how they are connected. For the same physical type different types of housing tenure may be used. For example, connected residences may be owned and leased by a single entity or may be owned separately by an agreement covering the relationship between units and common areas and concerns

WHAT IS RPM

A rental property is a residential or commercial property that is leased or rented for a given period of time to a tenant. There are short term rentals, such as vacation rentals, and long-term rentals, such as those on a one-to-three-year lease. Can also be explained to be A property from which the occupant(s), known as tenants, receives payment in exchange for the occupation or use of the house. The rental properties may be either commercial or residential. The rental property owner can be allowed to take other tax deductions, such as hypnotherapy interest and depreciation.

Now to explain what the management of this property will be, we can coin it as the management is the operation, control, maintenance and monitoring of residential and rental properties. This will include real estate, residential, industrial and immovable property. Management shows the need for the care and control of immovable property, with due regard for its useful life and condition. This is very similar to the role of manager in any organization.

A manager of rental properties is a individual or agency employed to supervise the day-to-day operations of a rental property unit. Rental property owners and developers of rental properties typically hire rental property managers when the assets themselves are unwilling or unmanageable. The cost of hiring a real estate manager is tax-deductible against the income generated from the land. Complex residences, shopping centers, and offices are growing types

of commercial property operated by managers of rental properties.

Intangible property defines properties that reflect existing or future value, but that, like stock and bond certificates, do not hold intrinsic value themselves. Although such things are merely pieces of paper, they can reflect considerable sums of money until stocks are redeemed, and bonds mature. Many forms of intangible property, such as the prestige of a company, are more nebulous, and a paper record can not be used to indicate this. Intangible properties are known as intellectual property, such as design principles, song lyrics, novels, and screenplays. Though such things are not of a physical nature, they may still be of considerable importance. Examples of intellectual property include the "swoosh" mark by Nike, and the Coca-Cola chemical formula. In order to maintain the ownership of intangible assets, individuals and companies usually employ attorneys to provide legal defense against infringement. When auditors, appraisers, and analysts calculate a business' worth, all of the underlying property is factored into the calculation. For example, a manufacturer of small machine parts that only gain $80,000 a year, but if it owns the factory it operates in and the building is valued at $1 million, the total value of the company will be considerably higher than the profit alone implies. Moreover, if the same company owns a patent on a product, it has the ability to gain significant revenue by selling the rights to sell the component to a larger corporation, rather than making the product in-house. In this way, licensing deals can build lucrative revenue streams that significantly boost the overall value of a company.

TERMINOLOGIES IS USED IN RPM

There are basic terminologies that will be explained so as to make the comprehension of this material easier for starters, and for those who are pros already, there would be no crime in refreshing one's mind. These terminologies are day to day terms used in the field of property management. Understanding or familiarizing oneself with these terminologies will make the learning journey easier and faster and of course more fun. Some of the terminologies that would be used in the course of this material are explained and highlighted below.

- Landlord-Tenant Law: A part of the Common Law which outlines the rights and duties of both landlords and tenants, including the duty to maintain the premises on the part of the tenant and the duty to provide the landlord with the possession.
- Proprietor Insurance: An insurance policy that protects the owner, such as burglary and burning, from financial risks associated with his rental property. The policy typically includes a number of optional coverage items; rent guarantee insurance, for example, and legal security.

- Investment Property: A property that the owner purchases to produce income by renting out the property to tenants.
- Equity: A disparity between the selling value of the house and the cash balance owed to the lender holding the mortgage. Equity is the amount the property owner will earn until the mortgage is paid off.
- Escrow Account: An account opened by the broker to keep the real estate transaction funds until completion or cancelation is completed. Use this account will ensure that the seller has enough money after approval to finalize the transaction.
- Ethics / Professionalism: A system of applied moral ideas which guides daily professional behavior and decision taking.
- Eviction: A legal procedure for a individual being expelled from their current home. The causes include breach of the lease agreement, and unpaid rent or mortgage.
- Notice of eviction: A formal document from the landlord detailing the default of the tenant relating to the terms of the lease. Eviction notices are meant to notify tenants of an eviction case pending against them.
- Fair Housing Act: A federal statute that seeks to ensure that age, color, disability, family status, gender, ethnicity, sex, and

religion do not discriminate in the housing market.

- Fair Market Value (FMV): An agreed price that is achieved by well-informed buyers and sellers following negotiations guided by current market conditions.
- Fixed expense: an expense element that is independent of the rental income but is part of the operating budget of the property (e.g. whether you have a tenant or not you will have to pay the property taxes per year).
- Flat rent: A $dollar monthly or annual land maintenance fee.
- Homeowners Association (HOA): an association composed of homeowners living in a specific condominium complex, planned community, or subdivision for the intent of creating and implementing guidelines and rules in the building.
- Tenancy at Suffrage: a condition in which the occupant has no lease yet, under the consent of the landlord, occupies the house. For example, after the end of the contract, a homeowner continues to live in the house, and the owner accepts daily rent payments. Often regarded at will as tenancy.
- Rental rate: An amount of money that tenants have to pay to landlords for renting a property for a fixed time span.

- Repairs: An operation to repair the property's missing or outdated parts or any fixtures within the living room.
- Return on Investment (ROI): A calculation showing how much income an investor receives as a percentage of the investment expense on the investment property.
- Sales Agent / Salesperson: A person with a licensed real estate broker performing immovable activities.
- Section 8: A program that allows private landlords to rent property for eligible tenants of low-income history at fair market rates. The voucher system relies on U.S.-funded rental subsidies. Housing, and Urban Planning Agency.
- Security Deposit: A sum the landlord has received from the occupant to secure funds to cover any damage to the house.
- Single Family House (SFH): A one family home.
- Subletting: Renting a property to a third-party owner by an owner for a specified portion of the lease agreement with the tenant.
- Subsidy / subsidized: A government financial assistance allocated for a given community or individual, such as housing market access funds.

- Tenant: A person who occupies or temporarily owns a property, a building or a designated unit under a fixed term agreement with the landlord.
- Tenant Application: A request that a prospective renter has to fill out in case of interest for a specific rental property.
- Tenant Damages: Any damage that happens during the duration of the contract that is not considered usual wear and tear.
- Three-day Notice: A form of eviction notice used in some states requiring payment of unpaid rent within a span of three days or vacating the property as the sole alternative.
- Townhouse: A typically two or three-story house that is connected by a shared wall to matching homes.
- Turnkey Home: A residential real estate home that does not allow the buyer to make urgent investments and can be rented out immediately after purchase.
- Utilities: utilities given to property owners, including electricity, garbage, gas, sewage, and water.
- Principal: A person who appoints another person to represent him or her as agent.
- Property: A real estate asset that includes land and any permanent buildings that

surround it, such as houses or other constructions.

- Building inspection: A visual inspection of a property which must be carried out in a non-invasive manner by a trained professional.
- Property management agreement: An agreement that clarifies the operation, obligations, and fees that the owner and a property management company must sign.
- Property manager: A person managing an immovable property belonging to someone else. Property managers receive compensation for, among other tasks, dealing with payroll, repairs, and rent collection.
- Property Showing: A planned rendezvous allowing prospective tenants to make a walk-through tour of the house.
- Property taxes: A tax based on the value of the property, which is paid to the local government by the property owner.
- Income and Loss Statement: An annually produced financial report that indicates the real net profit before any taxes.
- Proration: The method of decomposing and dividing expenses proportionally based on the share of owning or renting a property by each party.

- Real estate: A part of land which may or may not have permanent structures attached, such as houses.
- Real Estate Agent: A licensed agent who rents assets and sells them.
- Real Estate Cycle: A mechanism that reflects immovable market cycles including recovery, growth, hyper supply, and recession. The real estate market cycle could but not necessarily mimic the broader economic cycles.
- Realtor: A licensed real estate agent who must be a member of the National Realtors Association.
- Rent Guarantee Coverage (Rent Default Coverage): an policy protecting the landlord in the event that a renter faces financial distress and defaults on his or her rental payments.
- Rent Collection: An action whereby the landlord or a property management firm undertakes to obtain the money from each occupant under the conditions set out in the lease agreement.
- Lessor: A landlord giving the tenant a loan.
- Long-term rental: A long-term lease is also described as something agreed upon over a year.
- Properties Low-Income Tax Credit (LITC): properties qualify for tax credits in exchange for signing a lease agreement

with qualifying tenants. The eligibility conditions are based on IRS, HUD and Department of Justice requirements.

- Maintenance: A paragliding term for regular activities holding the property in good condition.
- Market Rate: The price of a real estate transaction, which depends on the expected price of the seller and the willingness of the buyer to pay.
- Mortgage: a lending contract specified by a legal agreement that obliges the borrower to repay the loan as directed, whereas the lender has a conditional right of ownership of the mortgage as security for the loan.
- Net operating income (NOI): a pre-tax calculation reflecting all property income after excluding critical operating expenses without including amortization, capital expenses and depreciation.
- Operating Budget: A financial plan that forecasts the revenue of the property over a span of one year and is offset by different expenses.
- Proportion charge: A percentage decided of the total collectible income of the property for a land management fee
- Vacant Land: A property inside which lacks any persons and personal property.

- Vacancy rate: the ratio of vacancies to the total number of rental units in the house, city or other category of operations
- Housing assistance Payments (HAP) Contracts: HAP contracts enable private landlords on behalf of a low-income household to obtain rental housing help.
- Housing and Urban Planning (HUD): HUD is the United States; Housing, and Urban Planning Agency. The department primarily focuses on rising home ownership rates and access to affordable housing.
- HVAC: A hybrid heating, ventilation, and air-conditioning system designed to create comfortable indoor conditions.
- Income Rates: Government-set income levels serve both statistical and decision-making purposes. These are used for the calculation of the tax credit cap, for example.
- Interest: A portion of the interest paid by a borrower to use certain assets by the lender. Interest in real estate usually refers to mortgage interest rates which depend on the interest rate, credit report and score of the Federal Reserve and the business decisions of the lender
- Apartment: A residential unit built within a housing structure. Defined often as a leased living space, essentially excluding condominiums and similar residential units.

- Broker: A real estate industry specialist who buys and sells properties on behalf of others while earning a fee in the process. Brokers need a license and adequate qualifications to practice in their home state.
- CAP Rate: The rate of capitalization (CAP) reflects the expected rate of return on a real estate investment property with a view to assessing the value and profitability of the investment.
- Comparable (Comps): a component of a valuation technique that calculates a current asset's value by using a newly acquired asset close enough to imply the anticipated selling price.
- Condo / Condominium: A house with multiple units that the people who live inside can own. All the dwellers within the condominium own the common areas and facilities equally.
- Conventional Housing: A form of housing that remains within the housing norms of the region or the market rate limits.
- Co-Signer: A secondary signer on a lease or mortgage who verifies the identity of the principal signer and/or gives the lender or landlord additional security.
- Curb Appeal: A term which expresses the attractiveness of the visual look of the house as seen from the level of the street.

- Depreciation: loss of value due to functionality loss, economic obsolescence or physical wear.
- Duplex (House): A house built within the same frame to include two separate individuals or families. For example, if one family lives upstairs in the upper floor and the other downstairs, then it is a duplex.
- Equal housing opportunity: All American citizens, regardless of age, disability, gender, family status, nationality, race or sexual orientation, can have the opportunity to live in different housing communities

REAL ESTATE MANAGEMENT

Land and anything fixed, immovable, or permanently attached to it like appurtenances, buildings, fences, fixtures, upgrades, roads, shrubs and trees (but not growing crops), sewers, structures, utility systems, and walls. Title to immovable property normally includes air rights, mineral rights, and surface rights that can be purchased, leased, sold or transferred together or separately. Also called real estate or immovable property. We can also explain it as a property consisting of land and the buildings on it, along with its natural resources such as crops, minerals or water; immovable property of this nature; an interest in this (also) real estate object, (more generally) buildings or housing generally.

Real estate is both a tangible asset and an immovable type. Examples of real property include land, houses, and other facilities, plus the rights to use and enjoy the land, and all its facilities. Renters and leaseholders may have rights to inhabit land or buildings that are considered a part of their property, but these rights are not, strictly speaking, considered real estate themselves.

Real property is not the same thing as personal property, and should not be confused. Personal assets include intangible assets such as investments, as well as tangible assets such as furniture and fixtures such as a dishwasher. Even renters may also claim parts of a home as personal property, provided that you have purchased and installed the property with the permission of the lessor.

Real estate is real, that is, tangible, land-based property and everything on it, including buildings, flora and fauna and natural resources.

Immovable properties have three basic categories: residential, commercial and industrial.

Residential real estate is less costly and more feasible for individuals when it comes to finance, whereas commercial real estate is more profitable and secure.

Immovable properties offer income and capital appreciation as an investment.

You can invest directly in real estate – buying land or property – or indirectly by buying shares in publicly traded real estate investment trusts (REITs) or mortgage-backed securities (MBS).

Residential property may contain either a single-family structure or a multi-family structure that is available for occupation or non-business.

Residences may be categorized by neighboring residences and property, and how they are related. For the same physical form specific forms of housing tenure can be used. For example, connected residences could be owned and leased out by a single entity, or possessed separately with an agreement covering the relationship between units and common areas and concerns.

TYPES OF REAL ESTATE

There are four types of real estates:

Residential real estate; covers older structures as well as resale homes. The single-family homes are the most popular type. There are also condominiums, co-ops, townhouses, duplexes, triple-deckers, quadplexes, households of high value, multi-generational and holiday homes. Also comprises of undeveloped land, houses, condominiums, and town halls. The buildings may be single-family or multi-family homes, and may be property owned or leased.

Residences may be categorized by neighboring residences and property, and how they are related. For the same physical form specific forms of housing tenure can be used. For example, connected residences may be owned and leased by a single entity or may be owned separately by an agreement covering the relationship between units and common areas and concerns.

Major forms of Residential Real Estate

Attached / Multi-unit Houses

Apartment (American English) or flat (British) – a single unit in a multi-unit building. Apartment boundaries are generally defined by a perimeter of doors that are locked or lockable. Sometimes seen in buildings with several floors' apartments.

Multi-family house – often seen in detached buildings with multiple stories, where each floor is a separate apartment or unit.

Terraced house (townhouse or row house)-A number of single or multi-unit buildings in a continuous row with shared walls and no space to intervene.

Condominium (American English)-An apartment-like building or complex owned by individuals. Common grounds and common areas are jointly owned and shared within the complex. There are condominiums in the townhouse or row house style also in North America. The British equivalent is a flats block.

Cooperative (a. k. a. co-op) – A type of multiple ownership in which the residents of a multi-unit residential complex own shares in the cooperative corporation owning the property, giving each resident the right to occupy a particular apartment or unit.

Half-family housing

- Duplex-Two units with one wall connected.
- Detached Houses
- Detached house or separate single-family house
- Handy dwellings
- Mobile homes or residential caravans – a full-time residence that can be mobile on wheels (although not in practice).
- Houseboats-A home that floats
- Tents – Typically temporary, with only fabric-like material consisting of a roof and walls.

Commercial real estate; comprises malls and shopping centers, medical and educational buildings, hotels, and offices. Also Comprises of non-residential buildings, such as office buildings, warehouses and retail buildings. These buildings may be stand-alone or in shopping centers. Apartment buildings are often considered commercial although used for residential purposes. That's because they're owned for revenue generation. Commercial buildings are commercial buildings which include office buildings, warehouses, and retail buildings (e.g. convenience stores, 'big box' stores, and shopping malls). A commercial building may combine functions in urban locations, such as offices on levels 2-10, with retail on floor. These buildings can be called multi-use if space allocated to multiple functions is significant. Local authorities generally maintain strict commercial zoning regulations, and have the authority to designate any zoned area as such; a business must be located in a commercial area or area at least partially for commercial purposes.

Major forms of commercial properties

Commercial real estate is generally split into five categories:

- Office Buildings – This category includes single-tenant buildings, small specialist office buildings, skyscrapers in downtown, and all in between.
- Retail / Restaurant – This category includes highway front pad sites, single tenant retail buildings, small shopping centers in the neighborhood, larger centers with grocery store anchor tenants, "power centers" with large anchor stores such as Best Buy, PetSmart, OfficeMax, and so on, even regional and outlet malls.
- Multifamily-This category includes complexes of apartments or high-rise apartment buildings. Anything bigger than a fourplex is usually called commercial real estate.
- Land-In the direction of potential growth, this category involves investment assets on

undeveloped, raw, rural land. Or, with an urban area, pad sites and more, infill the land.

- Miscellaneous – This catch of all categories would include any other non-residential properties such as developments in hotel, hospitality, medical and self-storage, and many more.

Industrial real estate; includes construction and property manufacturing, as well as warehouses. The buildings may be used to research, produce, store and distribute goods. This type of real estate property also includes factories, industrial parks, mines, and fisheries. Typically such assets are larger in scale, and locations can provide connections to hubs such as rail lines and harbors. Certain buildings which distribute goods are considered commercial property. Classification is important because they handle the zoning, construction and sales differently.

Industrial real estate is an umbrella term for fabrication, manufacturing, research and development, storage and distribution. While industrial property is often overshadowed by glitzier sectors such as residential, commercial and retail, industrial property should not be ignored as an integral enabler of global trade and as a robust, revenue-generating asset class.

Industrial Real property makes the global economy hum. Well-located, high-quality industrial real estate keeps the supply chains around the world running, allows for trade and e-commerce, and ensures the efficient flow of goods from producers to markets.

The industrial real estate industry covers properties used by firms during the course of a business operation. These properties include offices, warehouses, garages, and distribution centers as examples. Industrial properties can provide docking bays in which trucks are able to load and unload items.

Major forms of Industrial real estate

Warehouse and distribution centers

These buildings are typically very large, with high ceilings (40 + feet) ranging from 50,000 square feet to hundreds of thousands. Standard are multiple loading docks and ample accommodation space for semi-trucks. Such warehouses are more equipped for warehousing than for distribution. There are many ways the that disparity will play out. For example, most general-purpose warehouses have a lower door-to-square footage ratio, as products are not moving in and out as often as they do. It also means that location matters less than what's stored in those spaces, which is what drives most of the variation. For example, one type of general-purpose warehouses is cold storage facilities that are fitted with freezers (typically used as a food distribution center, cold storage buildings have space to hold large quantities of frozen goods) and usually used to store perishable food products.

- Heavy manufacturing; Heavy manufacturing buildings are designed to produce goods or materials and are typically equipped with large, specialized equipment. Light construction typically does not require the same equipment and can be carried out in a smaller setting. These massive plants aim to manufacture heavy duty products and goods. Usually they have tens or even hundreds of thousands of square feet in usable space, along with powerful pieces of equipment, three-phase electric power, and plenty of space for trucks to load product. The exact machinery inside is usually tailored to the end user, so when taking on new owners or tenants, heavy manufacturing plants need to be renovated. Consider Austral USA, the massive shipbuilding facility in Mobile, AL. If someone else wanted to take over this factory and use it to build, say, cars, the equipment would need to be changed accordingly.

- Light assembly; These spaces tend to be much smaller than their heavy counterparts and much simpler. That's because the items are typically assembled from smaller pieces, processed, and ultimately shipped off for sale to consumers. As such, they can be reconfigured much more easily for different tenants.

- Truck terminal; On the other end of the continuum from general purpose warehouses are truck terminals, solely devoted to transport. They are simply intermediate sites where goods are loaded from truck to truck, with little or no storage space.

- Research and Development; Research and development refers to research and development, the process through which companies create new products and improve existing ones. R&D properties differ greatly depending on the occupant and what space they may use it. For example, Google's soon-to-open self-driving car project facility will be 53,000 square feet, featuring wide open, indoor spaces to test self-driving cars away from prying eyes, and being located near Detroit, home to some of the best auto talent in the country. The property requirements ideally suit the use case. Enterprises in the electronics or biotechnology industries may use R&D

facilities. Typically these spaces have office areas, laboratories, and testing facilities.

- Database Centers: Data centers are where companies put their data-holding equipment in place, keep their internet up and running, and enable cloud storage. They average about 100,000 square feet but can get much bigger, with a 6.3 million square foot facility in Lang fang, China being the largest in the world. The reason the size varies so greatly is that a lot of companies choose to lease space in data centers of third parties. These are specialized buildings that require a large amount of electricity to power computer systems and telecommunications switching devices.

- Showrooms: Showrooms usually have a combination of office space, warehousing space and, most importantly, showrooms. More than half of the space is typically devoted to exhibiting and selling products. A car dealership would be the most familiar example to most people, but there are several other types of business that need showroom space. Showrooms have retail space that can be up to 50 per cent of the building, part warehouse and part sales floors.

- **Land**; comprises vacant land, work farms, and ranches. Subcategories within vacant land include undeveloped, early development or reuse, subdivision and site assembly.

MANAGEMENT AGENTS

A property management company, also known as property managers, is employed by income-producing property owners or landlords to operate their property's day-to-day requirements. Agents or managers are required to oversee a wide variety of projects from residential investment property, industrial or complex structures, and land development projects. It is a duty of a property management agent to optimize the value and profit of an investment property. Daily duties could include some or all of the following: space available for advertising and marketing; rent collection and financial updating; lease execution and extension; compliance of lease terms and building rules; monitoring of repair and maintenance schedules; and regular and timely contact with current tenants. Agents may also be responsible for activities such as producing financial reports, expanding rental and lease facilities and assessing the property market. As a broker for tenants or property owners, as necessary by the law, agents should be licensed and knowledgeable of all local, state, and federal regulations and building codes.

Officers in property management benefit from college degrees in property management, business administration, real estate or other related fields, and from recognized professional designations.

A property manager is an individual or organization that is hired to supervise a real estate unit's day-to-day operation. Land owners and real estate developers usually employ property managers when the assets themselves are reluctant or unable to be managed. The cost of employing a property manager is tax-deductible against the property 's revenue generated. Complex homes, shopping centers, and business offices are growing forms of commercial property managed by property managers.

Property managers provide an perfect solution for investors who do not live in close proximity to their rental properties or simply do not like dealing with tenants, toilets etc. There are several real estate investors, especially institutional real estate investors, who do not wish to be hands-on with investment.

STAFFING RESPONSIBILITIES

The duties of the property manager might include managing and organizing building maintenance and work orders, performing light handy and cleaning work, addressing tenant concerns and complaints, advertisement, showing and leasing vacant units, collecting and depositing rent, and periodically interacting with the property owner about the property's status. The property manager is the owner's eyes and ears on the property making sure problems are dealt with quickly and the property itself is properly cared for. Typical duties expected from a property manager include finding / evicting and dealing with tenants in general, and coordinating with the wishes of the owner. Such arrangements may require the property manager to collect rents, and pay necessary expenses and taxes, report to the owner on a regular basis, or the owner may simply delegate specific tasks and deal directly with others.

A property manager can arrange for a fee for a wide range of services, as may be requested by the property's owner. Where a dwelling (holiday home, second home) is occupied only periodically, the property manager could arrange for increased security monitoring, house-sitting, storage and shipping of goods, and other local sub-contracting necessary to make the property comfortable when the owner is in residence (services, operating systems, supplies and personnel on hand, etc.). Property management may also include commercial properties where the property manager is allowed to operate the business, as well as the property management. Some jurisdictions may require the licensing of a property manager for the profession.

The property manager is solely responsible to the owner and is secondary to the department. The property manager 's relationship with the landlord and the tenant is crucial in shaping both parties' expectations of the lease, since both parties will seek and expect certain rights and benefits from it.

The duties of the property manager may include managing and organizing building repairs and job orders, performing minor handy and cleaning jobs, addressing resident issues and grievances, advertisement, exhibiting and leasing empty apartments, receiving and depositing rent, and periodically speaking with the property owner on the property 's condition. The property manager is the owner's eyes and ears on the property making sure issues are handled promptly and the property itself is professionally cared for.

In general, when the landlord or real estate investor wishes to outsource some or all of the daily responsibilities of their rental property, a property manager is hired. In fact, property manager responsibilities can include a few basic tasks or you may be responsible for entire property operations.

We will go ahead and list 10 common manager's responsibilities below;

Finding New Tenants

Responsibilities for the property manager normally include tenant management. This is landlords' primary responsibility and many are glad to outsource this to property managers. The tenant management often includes finding tenants and attracting them. Residential real estate managers are expected to fill the property's vacant rental units. Therefore marketing of a rental property is part of the job description. They will need to advertise the rentals and post compelling advertisements to relevant listing sites and other advertising rental locations.

Tenant Screening

Property manager responsibilities also include ensuring that there is confidence in new prospective tenants. Here, professional property managers often have a particular tenant screening process that goes through the credit history and backgrounds of the prospective tenants. The good thing here is that the more people they screen over time, the better and faster they can pick the right tenants and avoid frequent tenant turnover.

Finding tenants: Property managers are charged with filling vacancies. They 're going to advertise the rent and create a compelling ad. They also understand what attracts tenants, allowing them to offer tips to help make the property.

Screening Tenants: Property managers should have a consistent screening process, including on-going credit checks and criminal background checks, which may lower your tenant turnover opportunities. Hundreds, even thousands, of tenants have been seen by experienced property managers, so they have a better idea of how to select the right tenants; those who will pay their rent on time, have a longer tenancy, and create fewer problems.

Handling Leases: This can include setting the term of the lease and ensuring that it has all the clauses necessary to protect the owner. That includes determining the amount of deposit required for security.

Handling Complaints / Emergencies: The property manager may handle requests for maintenance, noise complaints and emergency situations.

Handling Move Outs: The manager is responsible for inspecting the unit when a tenant moves out, checking for damages and determining what portion of the security deposit will be returned to the tenant. They are responsible for cleaning the unit, repairing any damage and finding a new tenant after they move out.

Dealing with Evictions: When a tenant fails to pay rent or otherwise breaches the terms of a lease, the property manager understands the proper way to file an expulsion and move forward.

Securing the Property

At the rental home, the duties of the property manager also go beyond routine maintenance. They would also need to protect the property either by hiring security guards or by installing adequate surveillance equipment, or both. Its function will also include developing policies and procedures to develop emergency preparedness. A professional property manager is aware that the more secure the property is, the more security the tenants feel. This enhances tenant retention.

Property Maintenance

Property manager responsibilities also include maintenance of properties. This will ensure the property remains in good condition and is a safe place for tenants. Maintenance means investigating and resolving complaints by tenants, and enforcing occupancy rules. They will also check all the vacant apartments and maintain and renovate them or coordinate contractors' work as needed. Note that basic maintenance can even include contracting snow removal services at colder locations.

Setting, Collecting, and Adjusting Rents

Rent collection is a basic obligation to every estate holder. Hence, property manager responsibilities can also include lease management as this task is gladly outsourced to property managers by landlords. In general, the property manager will also define and set up rent collection systems from tenants. They will often have to include strict deadlines and penalties for late payments, and there has been a method of checking all rents as agreed. Furthermore;

Setting Rent: The property manager would set the right level of rent for your property to attract tenants. The property manager will look at the market where the property is located to assess the rent price, and will evaluate similar properties in the city.

Collecting Rent: A system for collecting rent from tenants is set up by the property manager. They will set a date to collect rent each month and strictly enforce late fees to ensure optimum cash flow.

Rent adjustment: In accordance with individual state and/or municipal law the property manager can increase the rent each year. They can even lower the rent if they decide it's required.

In addition to collecting the rents, the property manager is also usually responsible for setting a rental rate. This needs that they learn the competition effectively. A property manager must adjust the rents to attract tenants but generate rental income for the owners as well. Similarly, the property manager can also raise or decrease the annual rent depending on changes in the real estate industry.

Coordinating Tenant Turnover

The responsibilities of property managers include the coordination of the tenant turnover. House owners are usually the ones who ought to plan as people come in and out. After former renters, property owners will have to search the rental spaces for vandalism, schedule maintenance and repair any violations before new tenants move in.

The property manager manages the evictions in some cases where renters cause problems. This means that they should know the laws of landlord-tenant as well as have the courage to handle the situation with confidence.

Handling Complaints

Maintenance and handling of complaints are also common responsibilities in property management. For example, if someone has frequent parties at the property and the neighbors complain about it, the property manager will probably be the one to deal with it. Sometimes property managers even have to deal with emergency situations, so you should be aware of the property's security precautions as well.

Staying Up-to-Date and Enforcing Landlord-Tenant Laws

Professional property managers need to have in-depth knowledge of local landlord tenant laws regarding screening tenants, handling security deposits, lease terminations and evictions, as well as compliance with property safety standards. They would have to follow this and all of the regulations outlined in the lease agreements. This may also include confronting potential infringers.

Overall Supervision

A property manager's duties and their position can sometimes be far more than one that meets the eye. Yes, the responsibilities of property managers do include the more visible day-to-day errands and services, but they can actually run the entire show in the background. That's if the real estate investor wants to use the entire spectrum of available property management support out there. Property managers may be asked to perform all the property analysis, planning, and management. To this end, they need a broad variety of management skills and real estate domain knowledge.

For example, if there are other workers employed in the rental house, security guards, property manager responsibilities require supervision of their jobs. That includes setting their wages and assessing their performance. Land owners will also supervise other future real estate contractors

PROPERTY MANAGEMENT INFORMATION PROFILE

Financial management starts from analyzing and setting the right rental rates, calculating costs, depreciation, and taxes for a residential property manager, as well as determining realistic profit goals and a budget to reach them. A property manager is also expected to achieve financial objectives, in addition to planning. To this end, they are collecting leases and paying invoices, tracking variances and taking corrective steps to get the budget back on track.

The profile of a property management firm basically indicates what and how they do what they do it shows information on how they run their schedules, gives a client a vague information on what thy have to offer, deals, properties available, how long they have been in business and what working like them will look like. Its like an information catalogue of a property management firm.

CHAPTER 2
LEASING AND OCCUPANCY POLICIES

More policies will keep coming up as we keep identifying the basics of this subject matter to enlighten us and broaden our knowledge spectrum on property management. let us define some terms to enhance comprehension and understanding.

A lease is a contractual arrangement in which the lessee (user) is required to pay the lessor (owner) for the use of an asset. Property, buildings, and vehicles are common leased assets. They also lease industrial or business equipment.

Broadly put, a lease agreement is a two-party contract between the lessor and the lessee. The lessor is the asset's legal owner; the lessee obtains the right to use the asset against regular rental payments. The lessee also agrees to adhere to different conditions relating to their use of the property or equipment. A person leasing a car, for example, may agree that the car would only be used for personal use.

A residential lease or rental agreement is a tenancy's blueprint: it sets out the landlord's and tenants' rights and responsibilities. Not only is it a contractual lease the parties can execute in court; it is also a highly detailed agreement full of

important financial specifics, such as how long the renters will use the property and the amount of rent owed per month.

The rules that landlords and renters consent to meet in their leasing arrangement are laid out in a lease or tenancy agreement. It is a legal contract, as well as an incredibly realistic paper full of crucial business specifics, like how long the occupant will occupy the property and the amount of rent due each month. Whether the lease or rental agreement is as short as one page or longer than five, typed or handwritten, it needs to cover the basic terms of the tenancy we can also explain a residential lease or rental agreement as the blueprint of a tenancy: It lays out the rights and responsibilities of both the landlord and the tenants. Not only is it a contractual lease the parties can execute in court; it is also a highly detailed agreement full of important financial specifics, such as how long the renters will use the property and the amount of rent owed per month.

Occupancy Leases means all leases, rental agreements and other occupancy agreements for the use or occupancy of any portion of the Property, if any, other than the Real Property and Rights Leases, together with all modifications, modifications, renewals and extensions thereof and all Tenant Deposits.

For commercial property owners and administrators, one of the key financial goals is to make sure that their land earnings improve.

A lease is a legal contract, and is thus enforceable by all parties under the applicable jurisdiction's contract law.

Because it also represents a conveyance of possessory rights to real estate in the United States, it is a hybrid kind of contract involving the qualities of an act.

Any particular forms of leases can have different provisions imposed by statute depending on the leased property and/or the state in which the arrangement was signed, or the parties' home.

Elements of a lease agreement

- Names of the contracting parties;
- Date and duration of commencement of the agreement.
- Identifies the particular object being leased (by street address, VIN, or make / model, serial number).
- Provides the renewal or non-renewal conditions.
- Is there a specific consideration (lump sum, or periodic payments) for the use of that object?
- Has security deposit provisions, and return terms.
- Can include a full set of conditions listed therein as Default Conditions and Full Remedies.
- Certain relevant requirements can be put upon the parties such as:
- Need to provide insurance for loss.
- Restrictive use.
- Which party is responsible for maintenance?
- Termination clause (describing what will happen if the contract is ended early or cancelled, stating the rights of parties to terminate the lease, and their obligations)

Contents of the Occupancy lease policy:

Understanding what a lease policy looks like and what it should contain is paramount knowledge for both professionals, or just investors. Here are some contents expected to be seen and identified in an occupancy document;

Name All tenants and employees in your rental or lease agreement

Any adult living in the rental — including both members of a married or unmarried couple — must be named as a tenant and sign the rental or lease agreement. Requiring all adult residents to be official tenants is a form of extra landlord insurance: each resident is lawfully responsible for paying the entire rent price and subject to the other provisions of the lease or tenancy agreement. That ensures you will legitimately claim the entire rent from all of the tenants if one tenant skips out and refuses to pay the rent. Also, if one tenant breaches the lease or rental agreement, you are entitled to terminate all tenants' tenancy—not just the offender. This also renders an occupant legitimately responsible for all terms including the full rent sum and reasonable use of the land. This means that you can legally seek the entire rent from any of the tenants should the others skip out or be unable to pay; and if one tenant breaches a significant term of the agreement, you can terminate the tenancy on that lease or rental agreement for all tenants.

It is also a good idea to add an occupancy clause stating that only tenants and their minors are allowed to reside in the rental, and that guests are allowed to stay no longer than a set number of days. Then, if a tenant moves or sublets the unit in an unapproved roommate without your permission, you have the right to terminate the tenancy and, if necessary, evict all residents.

Rental Property Description

Require the whole property address (including, where applicable, building and unit number). You'll also want to note any particular storage areas or parking spots included. For example, if the rental includes assigned car park, please be sure to write in the number of the stall or spot. Similarly identify places not open to renters (such as a closed shed in the backyard).

Terms of Tenancy

Rental agreements create short-term (usually month-to-month) tenancies that renew automatically until the landlord or tenants terminate. Leases, on the other hand, create tenancies that terminate after a specific term (usually a year). Whichever you use, be specific: note the start date, the tenancy length, and (if creating a lease) the expiration date. This also indicates that Each rental document should state whether this is a rental contract or a fixed-term lease. Rental agreements usually run from month to month, and renew themselves unless the landlord or tenant has terminated them. Conversely, leases typically last one year. Your choice will depend on how long you want the tenant to stay and how flexible your arrangement is.

Occupancy levels/limits

Your agreement should specify clearly that the rental unit is the residence of only the tenants who signed the lease and their minor children. This guarantees the right to decide who lives in the house-preferably, people you have screened and accepted-and to restrict the number of inhabitants. The value of this clause is that, without your permission, it gives you reason to evict a tenant who moves in a friend or relative, or who sublets the unit.

Cost to pay

Don't just write in the amount of the rent — spell out when (typically the first of the month) and how it's going to be paid to your office, for example by mail. (Make sure that you comply with the rent payment laws of your State.) To avoid confusion, describe details such as:

- Acceptable methods of payment (for instance personal check only)
- Whether you are charging a late rent fee, the fee and the grace period (if any), and
- Any fees in case the rent checks bounce.

Leasing Deposits and Maintenance Payments

By being quite transparent about your transactions and agreement you can prevent some of the most frequent conflicts between landlords and tenants:

- The dollar value of the safe deposit (sure if you abide by certain state security deposit cap laws)
- How to use the deposit (e.g. to cover unpaid rent or repair damage caused by the tenant) and how not to use it (e.g., you will not accept it instead of last month's rent)
- That you want the tenant to replenish the deposit in case you are forced to make a mid-tenancy deduction (for example, if you replace a window the tenant's child throws a ball into the tenancy for two months)
- When and how the deposit and deduction account will be returned after the tenant moves out (check the laws of your State on returning security deposits) and
- Any non-refundable fees, for example for cleaning or pets (ensure that your state allows non-refundable fees).

It is also a good idea (and legally required in a few states and cities) to include details about where the security deposit will be held and whether you will pay interest on the tenant's deposit. Many tenants may need at least a security or risk deposit for the owner to rent the home, but there are other fees and costs that you will like to add in the lease, such as a pet deposit or a late rent fee. Note that there is a difference between a deposit and a fee: a deposit is refundable, which means that if they move on, you will be obliged to return the amount to your tenant, unless there are specific reasons for you not to return that money. For example, a damage deposit is meant to restore damage done by the tenant when they leave, and if a tenant damages the house, then the full amount will be withheld to pay maintenance expenses or only a part will be refunded.

A charge is usually not refundable, but when relating to payments and deposits in your contract be sure you use the right language.

Maintenance and repair policies

Your best defense against rent-withholding problems and security deposit battles is to explain your repair and maintenance policies clearly, for example, you could include a clause that says your tenant should keep the suite clean and free from the buildup of garbage.

As another example, you could state that without your permission, your tenant should not make changes to the suite, such as installing an alarm system or painting the walls.

Keep in mind that landlords are usually responsible for habitability-dealing repairs, such as heating or plumbing. Some other policies could include;

- Responsibility of tenants to maintain safe and hygienic premises and compensate for any harm they inflict (excluding usual wear and tear)

- The requirement that the tenants notify you of defective or dangerous conditions, with specific details of your complaint handling and repair requests procedures and
- Restrictions on tenant repairs and alterations (for example, prohibit any unit painting unless you give written approval).

Landlord Right to access Land

To avoid claims by tenants for illegal entry or infringement of privacy rights, your lease or rental agreement should clarify your right to access the rent. It's okay (if allowed under the landlord access laws of your state) to have different policies for different situations — for example, you may provide a 24-hour notice before entering to make repairs or show the unit to potential renters, but you may not be able to give advance notice in an emergency.

Your Laws and Regulations

If you have such an important rule or regulation that you would want to remove a tenant who has violated it, be sure to include it. Other rules which are not so vital can be written in a separate document of rules and regulations. In their leases and rental agreements, the landlords commonly include the following policies:

No illegal activity: To limit your potential liability and help prevent injury to others and your property, you should include an explicit clause prohibiting illegal and disruptive behavior, such as drug dealing, drug use and excessive noise or nuisance.

Smoking: You have the right at your rental to prohibit or restrict smoking of any kind. If you do not allow smoking, you might want to note that all forms of smoking, including marijuana or vaping, are included in the prohibition. If you limit smoking, write down where and what tenants might be smoking to.

Pets: You have the right to restrict or prohibit pets in your rental, except for animals that provide emotional support and service. If your tenancy is pet-friendly, provide your pet policy: write down how many pets a resident can have and define the forms, breeds and animal sizes that you require. Note also if pets have to be on leash outside the unit, or if tenants have to clean up pet waste in common areas or yards.

Contact details

Your residential lease should include the names and contact information of all persons residing in the rental unit (such as personal and work phone numbers and email addresses); Consider requiring tenants to contact you regarding certain matters in writing. Although text and instant messaging may work for some discussions, you want to be able to keep a record of all communications with your tenants reliable — and printable, in case you ever need to show a judge.

For example, by sending a letter to a designated address you might state that tenants must request repairs in writing or give notice to terminate the tenancy. If you agree to accept email, please make sure you check email regularly and have methods to save (and back up) everything you send and receive.

Rent Amount and Frequency

Your residential lease has to include how much rent the tenant has to pay, and how often. The tenant usually pays rent on a monthly basis but sometimes, depending on the tenancy term, landlords offer the tenant the option of paying annually. Allowing the client to pay upfront could be worthwhile if they can have the peace of mind that their rent is taken care of in the case of a financial disaster.

Rent amounts can change over time, depending on a number of factors such as higher utility costs or property tax. How you raise rent amounts for your property differs depending on the type of lease you signed with your landlord. Many times, if you intend to increase the price of the rent, you need to contact the client in writing with a Notice of Rent Raise.

Other Listing restrictions on the rental agreement

You may be required by federal, state, and local law to disclose certain information in your lease or rental agreement. You would need to warn tenants about lead-based paint, for example, or the history of bed bug of the building. You will also want to ensure that your lease or rental agreement does not infringe any laws on rent control, anti-discrimination laws or health and safety codes. Consider having your lease or rental agreement reviewed by a local landlord-tenant lawyer to ensure it complies with all applicable laws.

TYPES OF LEASE DOCUMENTS

A lease is an implicit or written arrangement that lays out the terms on which a lessor agrees to allow a property to be used by a lessee. The agreement promises the use of the property by the lessee for an agreed length of time, while the owner is guaranteed consistent payment over the agreed period. Both parties are bound by the terms of the contract, and if either fails to fulfill the contractual obligations there is a consequence.

Leases differ widely but in the real estate sector there are some that are common. The structure of a lease is influenced by the preference of the lessor, as well as by current market trends. Some leases put a tenant 's burden while others put the entire load over to the property owner. Not all of that; there are a number of different forms in there. The most common forms of tenancy agreements are presented here.

1. Full Net Lease: The tenant takes care of the entire burden in an absolute net lease including

insurance, taxes and maintenance. The absolute form is typical in single-tenant schemes where the property owner builds accommodation units to match a tenant's needs. For a specified duration the proprietor turns over the finished unit to the tenant. In such a situation, the tenants typically involve big corporations who recognize the terms of the deal and are able to share the outlays. However, since most of the burden lies with the tenant, property owners generally accept lower monthly rates.

2. Triple Net Lease: The triple net lease is associated with three expense categories: insurance, maintenance and real-estate taxes. Such expenses are also known as pass-through or operating expenses because they were all passed on to the tenant by the property owner in the form of excess rents. The excesses are sometimes referred to as taxes, insurance, and common area (TICAM).

Triple net agreements, often referred to as NNN, are the norm in single-tenant and multi-tenant leasing units. The tenant exercises control over the landscaping and exterior maintenance under a single tenant lease. In short, as long as the tenancy is in effect the tenant decides what the property looks like.

A multi-tenant contract provides absolute power over the design of a property to the proprietor. No tenant can ruin the overall look of a building in such a way. Moreover, a multi-tenant arrangement requires that the tenant pay a regular pro-rata to the operating costs.

For this reason tenants are granted the right to audit the operating costs of the building. A triple net lease precludes the owner of the property from hiring a concierge. Each tenant contributes to the costs for the maintenance of the buildings and the interior.

3. Modified Gross Lease: The modified gross lease transfers all the burden to the landowner. The owner pays all insurance, property taxes as well as maintenance of the common area on the basis of the conditions. On the other hand, the tenant shoulders the costs of janitorial maintenance, utility, and interior maintenance.

The tenancy arrangement also stipulates that the owner bears responsibility for the roof and other structural aspects of the building. However, since the owner takes care of a large portion of the cost of the tenancy, the monthly rates are higher than in other types.

The modified type of lease is advantageous for the tenant as the owner will take care of associated risks such as operating costs. The prices for the occupant are generally the same over the year, and he takes no role in the property's affairs. Unfortunately, each month the owner may choose to charge a premium to cater for the building management costs.

4. Full Service Lease: The full-service lease, as the name suggests, takes care of most of the costs of running a building. However, there are a few exceptions to this, such as data and telephone costs. Otherwise, the rest of the costs are for the property owner, including the maintenance of the common area, taxes, interior, insurance, utility, and janitorial costs. The monthly rent is therefore marginally high, and these leases are popular in big multi-tenant units where partitioning a building into smaller spaces is impractical.

Such an agreement is favorable for the homeowner, as there are no extra expenses above the normal monthly rent. The disadvantage is that the owner may choose to charge a small premium on top of the monthly rate to cover the tenancy costs. Most owners prefer the full-service arrangement, since it allows total control over the overall appearance of a building.

Essentially, there are different types of leases but absolute net lease, triple net lease, modified gross lease, and full-service lease are the most common types. Tenants and landlords need to thoroughly recognize them before a tenancy agreement is signed.

Similarly, both property owners and tenants benefit enormously if they engage real estate experts during such agreements. Experts in real estate are the best people to talk to, since they can give the best advice when leasing property.

SOCIAL SERVICE REQUIREMENTS

Before we go into social working being a field in property management, let us understand the concept itself on its own.

Social services are a range of government, private, profit, and non-profit - making public services. These public services aim at creating more efficient organizations, building stronger communities and promoting equal opportunities. Social services include benefits and facilities such as education, food subsidies, health care, police, fire service, employment training and housing subsidies, adoption, community management, policy research, and lobbying.

Social service workers, also known as social workers, can be professionals who are certified, registered or licensed to help people deal with problems that affect their daily lives. These issues may include drug abuse, injury or disease, domestic violence, psychological or mental problems, or lack of appropriate housing and other social services. Many of these client issues are of a very serious nature, and can be difficult to handle on a daily basis. Some social work organizations are understaffed, which could result in additional stress on the workers. Social service workers often have to travel to the homes of clients to meet with them or conduct inquiries.

Most people with a career in social services get personal satisfaction from assisting people throughout their working day. Most careers in the social services demand compassion and dedication. Staff in the support sector play an significant role in the lives of individuals.

Careers in social services attract people who enjoy helping people, who want to help people make their lives better. People with jobs in social work usually help people operate in their community the best they can.

Many positions in social services require a bachelor's degree, and some positions in social services can require a graduate-cert. Some of the degree programs include study in the classroom, and practical experience in the field. Some careers in social services require that people be licensed, certified, or registered. Requirements vary according to career and state in the social services.

How to become a social worker.

Earn a Degree in Social Work.

Social service workers generally get a Bachelor's degree in Social Work (BSW) or a Master's degree in Social Work (MSW) through a program that is accredited by the Social Work Education Council

(CSWE). Some programs allow students to focus on specific areas of social work, such as individual, child, family, organizational, or practice in community. Courses may include classes in theory and practice of social work, human behavior, social diversity, family law and policy, child welfare, and substance abuse.

Volunteering or interning to get practical experience

Aspiring social service workers who complete bachelor's programs can benefit from taking part in volunteer and internship opportunities while in school. Students can serve in local human rights organizations, outreach programs or similar institutions to gain hands-on experience working with needy people. In some cases, volunteer or internship experience is required to earn a Social Work degree.

Gain Work Experience.

Social workers with a bachelor's degree can find employment opportunities in most social work positions in the direct service. They will identify client needs and skills as part of their everyday practice, respond to child endangerment or public welfare emergencies, review treatment strategies, direct clients to community services, and help clients apply for federal assistance. For MSW holders an internship or other supervised experience is required. MSW program graduates can gain experience in social work through fellowships. Fellowships that can last for 9-24 months provide supervised experience for graduates working with patients in a clinical setting. In general, this post-MSW work experience is required for obtaining state licensing.

Obtain a State License.

States have different licensing requirements for workers in the social services. The designation of Licensed Clinical Social Worker (LCSW) is usually reserved for social workers with an MSW who have completed an assessment given by the Social Work Boards Association and fulfilled professional experience and other qualifications criteria. The state certificate of a social worker must be renewed periodically, depending on the requirements of each Jurisdiction

Consider Earning a Credential.

The National Social Workers' Association (NASW) maintains three certification rates. The basic professional credential is the designation of the Academy of Certified Social Workers (ACSW), available to qualified candidates with an MSW, at least two years of supervised postgraduate employment in social work, and 20 additional hours of related continuing education. The NASW also provides the Qualified Clinical Social Worker (QCSW) credential for applicants who are already members of the ACSW, hold a current state social work license and an MSW, have at least three years of supervised postgraduate clinical employment and 30 hours of continuing clinical social work training. Among other eligibility requirements, the highest designation of the organization is the Diplomate in Clinical Social Work (DCSW), which requires current QCSW certification and an additional three years of full-time experience performing clinical social labor.

Maintain Credentials.

Social workers are required to periodically renew their professional licenses and certifications, and renewal is commonly required for continuing education. Via specialized courses and educational workshops, social workers will continue their studies and learn new skills and strategies that aid with their practice. In addition, continuing education can help a social worker stay up-to - date with trends in industry and changes in social labor laws.

Join a Vocational Organization

Becoming a member of a professional organization such as NASW can provide access to a variety of benefits for social services workers to continue their careers. Some of the benefits might include resources for professional development, networking opportunities and access to options for continuing education.

Social service workers, also known as social workers, must obtain at least a bachelor's degree in social work, psychology, sociology, or related fields; although they must have a master's degree in clinical social labor. There is also a general requirement for two years of training and a state license.

Social workers

Disasters have disproportionate impacts on some subpopulations as a result of pre-existing conditions in societies, especially those of low socioeconomic status and other disadvantaged groups. Loss of meager resources, exacerbation of pre-existing health conditions, and higher rates of prior trauma can lead to poor health outcomes in poorer groups, including increased incidence of substance abuse and mental

distress. Professionals in social services act as advocates and service providers for underserved populations, enabling people to access critical goods and services, and become healthier and more self-sufficient. Social services can help to mitigate the impacts of disasters on vulnerable populations by ensuring access to the needed resources.

Unfortunately, until recently the social care system has been widely removed from preparedness and emergency response measures. Events such as Hurricane Katrina that had devastating effects on vulnerable populations have shown the importance of integrating social services into all other recovery activities including, but not limited to, delivery of clinical care, housing, economic and labor development, and transportation.

In light of that let us briefly see how social workers are making a recovery around these loose ends;

- Build on established partnerships and establish detailed strategic strategies among social care funders and providers, civic and religious groups, and advocates to ensure integrated provision of social services across all phases of disaster preparation and recovery.
- Integrate recovery plans for social services into other services for recuperation of disasters.

- Establish consistent processes, policies, and procedures to facilitate financing and information flow through federal, state, and local networks.
- Provide support for reuniting families and encouraging resilience through community programming designed to strengthen networks of social support.
- Focus on restoring normalcy through key services / activities in the community, such as child care, elder care, foster care, mental health services, schools, housing, jobs, and transport.
- Improve efforts to increase transparency to serve the most vulnerable populations to provide the social services that are needed.
- Promoting continued assessment and lifelong development to promote programs of social care and meet goals for the health system.

CITIZENSHIP PROCEDURES

Citizenship is the status of a person recognized as a legal member of a sovereign state or as belonging to a nation under custom or law. The idea of citizenship has been defined as individuals' ability to defend their rights before governmental authority. Individual states and nations recognize people's citizenship by their own policies, regulations, and criteria as to who is entitled to their citizenship. It is basically a relationship between an individual and a state that the individual owes loyalty to and, in turn, has the right to its protection. Citizenship implies the status of freedom with responsibilities accompanying it. Citizens have certain rights, duties and obligations which are excluded or applied only partly to aliens and other non-citizens resident in a region. In addition, full civil rights are predicated on citizenship, including the freedom to vote and to hold public office. Citizenship ordinary responsibilities are loyalty, taxation, and military service.

An individual can have multiple citizenships. An individual who has no citizenship in either State is considered to be stateless, while an individual whose territorial status is unknown is a border lander.

The most privileged type of nationality is citizenry. This broader term denotes different relationships between an person and a state which do not automatically grant political rights but imply other privileges, particularly security abroad. It is the term used in international law to describe all individuals covered by a State. Nationality often tends to indicate the relation to a state of persons other than individuals; for example, corporations, vehicles, and aircraft have a nationality.

First of all, the concept of citizenship arose in ancient Greece's towns and city-states, where it generally applied to property owners but not to women, slaves or the poorer community members. A citizen in a city-state in Greece had the right to vote, and was liable for taxation and military service. The Romans first used citizenship as an instrument for distinguishing Rome 's residents from those peoples whose territories Rome had conquered and incorporated. As their empire continued to grow, the Romans granted proper citizenship to their allies throughout Italy, and then to peoples in other Roman provinces, until it was extended to all free inhabitants of the empire in 212 CE. Within the empire Roman citizenship granted significant legal rights. During the Middle Ages, the idea of national citizenship in Europe practically vanished, substituted as it had been by a system of feudal privileges and obligations. In the late Middle Ages and the Renaissance, holding citizenship in various towns and cities of Italy and Germany became a guarantee of immunity for merchants and other privileged persons from the feudal overlords' claims and prerogatives. Modern concepts of citizenship crystallized during the American and French Revolutions in the 18th century, when the term citizen came to indicate the possession of certain freedoms in the face of the coercive powers of absolutist monarchs.

In England the term citizen originally referred to membership of a municipal borough or local corporation, while the word subject was used to emphasize the subordinate position of the individual relative to the monarch or state. The word subject is still used in British common-law usage and nationality laws in relation to the individual, but the two words are practically identical, because British constitutional monarchy is still a ceremonial one that has lost its previous legislative control over its subjects.

Birth within a given territory, descent from a citizen parent, marriage to a citizen, and naturalization are the main reasons for the acquisition of citizenship (apart from international transactions such as territorial transfer or option). There are two main systems used to determine citizenship from the time of birth: jus soli, by which citizenship is acquired through birth within the state territory, irrespective of parental citizenship; and jus sanguinis, by which a person, wherever born, is a citizen of the state if his or her parent is one at the time of birth. The United States and the British Commonwealth countries adopt the jus soli as their fundamental principle; they also acknowledge the acquisition of nationality by descent but subject it to strict limitations. Other countries generally adopt the jus sanguinis as their basic principle, supplementing it by provisions on the acquisition of citizenship in the case of a combination of birth and domicile within the country, birth within the country of parents born there, and so on. Nationality law requirements that overlap sometimes result in dual nationality; one person can be a citizen of two countries. Alternatively, the lack of uniform rules on the acquisition and loss of citizenship has occasionally led to a lack of citizenship (statelessness).

Acquisition of a woman's citizenship by marriage to a citizen was the prevailing principle in modern times until after World War I. Under this system, the wife and children shared the husband and father's nationality status as head of the family. From the 1920s, a new system developed under the impact of women's suffrage and ideas about men and women's equality, in which marriage did not affect a woman's nationality. The resulting mixed-nationality marriages often cause problems, particularly with regard to the children's nationality status, and subsequently various mixed schemes have been invented, both stressing the freedom of choice of the wife and child.

General ways of becoming a citizen are highlighted below

Citizenship by Naturalization

Naturalization refers to the process whereby a person who is not born in the United States voluntarily becomes a citizen of the United States. Naturalization is the most common way of becoming a US citizen for foreign-born persons. There are many conditions that have to be fulfilled before a person can apply for citizenship. In general, applicants must be 18 years old and fall into one of the following three basic categories of eligibility:

- 5 years as a permanent resident.
- 3 years as a permanent resident who has lived in marital union with a U.S. citizen spouse for at least 3 years.
- Qualifying service in the U.S. Armed Forces.

Citizenship by Derivation

When a parent naturalizes, his or her children (under 18 years old and at the time living with the parent) may automatically "derive" U.S. citizenship, provided they are also permanent residents. Moreover, a child who obtains U.S. citizenship by derivation does not have to participate in a ceremony for naturalization. Generally, if three requirements are met, foreign-born children under 18 automatically acquire U.S. citizenship:

- The child must have U.S. lawful permanent resident status ("green card" holder); and
- At least one parent must be a U.S. citizen; and
- The child must be residing in the United States in the legal and physical custody of a U.S. citizen parent.

Citizenship by Acquisition

Under certain circumstances, a child is automatically "acquiring" citizenship even though that child was born outside the USA. At the time of the child's birth at least one parent must be a U.S. citizen, and several other conditions must be met. These children may also acquire U.S. citizenship at birth when that child marries and has children. The ways in which a child can become a citizen of the United States through acquisition generally include:

- Both parents were American citizens
- At the time of the child's birth, all parents were U.S. residents and the parents were married at the time of conception, and at least one parent lived in the U.S., or its territory, or both, until the child's birth.

- One parent was a United States resident
- One parent was a U.S. resident at the time of the birth of the infant; and the child was born on or after November 14, 1986; and the parents were married at the time of birth; and the U.S. citizen parent was physically present in the U.S. or its jurisdiction for at least five years at some point in his or her life before birth, at least two years after his or her 14th birthday.
- One parent was a United States resident
- One parent was a U.S. resident at the time of the birth of the infant; and the date of birth is before November 14, 1986, but after October 10, 1952; and the parents of the child were married at the time of birth; and the U.S. citizen parent was physically present in the U.S. or its jurisdiction for a span of at least ten years at some point in

his or her life previous to the birth of the child, at least five of whom were physically present in the U.S.

The benefits of being a citizen

let us briefly talk about the benefits of being a citizen of a country in relation to property management and ownership. The most important benefit is the right to vote in elections. In a democracy, citizens can play a big role in shaping the decisions a country makes. The desires and opinions of citizens can influence elected lawmakers. Since citizens have the right to vote, they can elect officials whose political ideas they share. If they are unhappy with an elected official, they can vote for someone else in the next election. People will run for political office themselves.

If you are a citizen you can file a motion to lawfully bring your mother, unmarried children who are minors, and husband or wife to the United States. Generally, they will get their permanent resident (or legal) status quickly. Citizens can also bring their adult children and brothers and sisters here, although getting permanent residence will take longer.

Having a U.S. passport allows citizens the freedom to travel. You can travel for long periods of time. You can also live outside of the United States. In addition, citizens receive U.S. Government security and support while overseas.

Citizenship in relation to owning properties can be tricky as each country run on different legal procedures. We will be addressing some of these different procedures for different countries how your citizenship status affects your property rights, policies and management.

Few issues in everyday life or politics are more important than what we have, and who we are. Property and citizenship are perhaps the most obvious and familiar manifestations of these core dimensions, in the broadest sense of the word. In their Constitution, land and citizenship are closely related. Reconnaissance is the core element of both. The processes of recognizing political identity as belonging and claims to land and other resources as property work simultaneously to imbue the institution that legitimizes and recognizes its authority to do so. These are, so to speak, the "contracts" that connect citizenship and property to political authority in society. Therefore, struggles over citizenship and property have as much to do with the scope and constitution of authority as with access to membership and resources. However, the groups of people entitled to seek entitlements aren't set in stone.

Land, more than most African issues, closely links the two aspects: land claims are partly defined by social identity, and social identity is partly defined by land ownership rights. In addition, I think this complex relation is broadly true for postcolonial societies – and it's a valuable intellectual entry point to power analysis in any society. Land is immediately important in Africa and other postcolonial societies for the livelihoods of large populations – rural and urban alike – and it forms an integral part of the social and economic development of the society. Increasing demand on land capital, land disputes and political activism is making land rights a critical political issue.

Citizenship is generally – but not always – organized as a relationship between individuals and a public authority institution, but it does not refer exclusively to national citizenship – this is just one of several forms. It is basically shorthand for the political subjectivity and agency of individuals, meaning that citizenship denotes by what political institution a person derives membership rights to that community. Land in Africa is a tool to which exposure is not just guaranteed by membership in a national group – local citizenship and status are also just as important or even more significant. Just as multiple sets of rules prevail and several institutions compete to exercise authority over rights allocation, so in most African societies belonging is also layered. We are debating and evolving the definition of citizenship in relation to property in Africa, arguing that although people have a national citizenship that endows them with certain privileges, it is not the only essential type of membership in a political class and the only source in privileges. One distinction appearing to be increasingly invoked in African and other societies is what we might call "national" and "local" citizenship. While people may share national citizenship, they often invoke the idea of autocracy – first arrival – as a mechanism of inclusion and exclusion. Citizenship-or membership in politics-implies, so to speak, rights to have rights.

CHAPTER 3
QUALITIES OR PROPERTY MANAGERS

Briefly discussing property managers as previously discussed above, property managers have a good option for owners who don't live close to their rental properties, who don't like dealing with renters, toilets etc. There are many property investors, especially institutional real estate investors, who don't want to be hands-on to the investment.

Property management officer benefit from college degrees in property management, business administration, immovable property or other related fields and recognized professional designations.

A property manager is an person or agency employed to oversee day-to-day operation of a real estate company. Land owners and real estate developers typically hire land managers when they are unable or unwilling to handle the properties themselves. The cost of hiring a real estate manager is tax-deductible against the income generated by the land. Increasing forms of commercial property managed by property managers are complex homes, shopping centers, and business offices.

A property management agency, also known as property managers, is hired by income-generating property owners or landlords to handle the day-to-day needs of their properties. Agents or managers are expected to supervise a broad number of residential investment property projects, commercial or complex structures, and land development projects. The optimization of the value and profit of an investment property is a duty of a property management agent. Daily duties could include some or all of the following: space available for advertising and marketing; rent collection and financial updating; lease execution and extension; compliance with lease terms and building rules; monitoring of repair and maintenance schedules; and regular and timely contact with existing tenants. Agents may also be responsible for activities such as financial reporting, rental and lease expansion, and property market assessment. As a broker for tenants or property owners, agents should be licensed and knowledgeable of all local, state, and federal regulations and building codes as required by law.

Now the question is, how would you know a good agent, how would you be able to identify a goo property manager who has the skill set of managing your properties without causing any form of inconveniences. A property manager needs to be able to listen and communicate, and to be proactive and engaged, up-to - date and knowledgeable. He or she should be level-headed, resourceful, personable and articulate as well. The list of "and's" continues and goes on for all the property managers diligently trying to excel. However, at the end of the day, most professionals working in the management sector believe that the most important characteristic a good property manager needs to possess is the capacity to interact and respond to individuals. Here are some highlighted qualities you should look out for when hiring a property manager;

Communication is important

Good communication is the grease in wheels of a building. It is the duty of the property manager to ensure that everything is running smoothly, and that requires that everyone involved in the building understand each other. Conflict is generally the result of misunderstandings, often precipitated by a lack of communication or a breakdown. A property manager, like a good foreign diplomat, needs to be able to see the perspectives of other peoples, hear what they're saying and solve problems. The property manager must consider and align the views of various stakeholders. "It is very important that a property manager is a good listener, who is detail-oriented and follow-up. In addition, a property manager must be able to listen, then understand and interpret what the unit owners [or shareholders], the super manager, the board of directors and so on are telling him or her.

For everyone associated with the building, the property manager is the go-between, so as Gold mentions, they need to be a good interpreter and exhibit diplomacy: listening, understanding and translating messages between different parties. You may want to take a closer look at your manager if you are a member of your board and you have had problems with the super or the doorman, or if the unit owners have been complaining.

A Field of Intelligence

A good property manager not only communicates well but also keeps the board of directors informed on several different levels, financially and otherwise. According to Greg Cohen of Impact Management in Queens, "A managing agent should provide two monthly reports — a financial report ... and a physical report that covers the building's day-to-day operations." The annual statements will consist, according to Cohen, of a general ledger displaying the estimated and the real budget, as well as of accounts payable status reports on creditors or unit members. It should also include a check register showing all the money paid out for the month, as well as copies of bills, bank statements, checks and a bank reconciliation. In short, the property manager should provide ALL financial information that they require to the board.

The second report should consist of all correspondence between management, tenants / owners, board, etc., and any other paperwork with respect to the operations of the building. By keeping the board of directors updated on a monthly basis, the manager can ensure the board is informed and prepared, and is therefore less likely to be caught unaware by any unpleasant surprises. In cities where laws are constantly changing and new laws are constantly being drawn up, a property manager needs to stay up-to - date with the emerging regulations. They have to be reading the newspapers, keeping an eye out for new laws that could affect their construction. In addition, each manager has to manage the approaching deadlines (for inspections, just to name one example) and bring relevant information to the attention of the board.

This, that, and first, people.

A property manager's work is a juggling act that allows the agent to foresee and address the building's administrative problems without losing sight of the obligation of all the building's men. A property manager is accessible with PDAs, cell phones, and e-mail almost all of the time — for better or worse. One of the main criticisms about property managers today, according to Cohen, is that they don't answer phone calls. They are in charge of equipment, budgets, staff, specialists, boilers, and a whole slew of tasks that require outstanding management and multi-tasking skills, but eventually they have to be able to answer questions and handle individuals.
"Some homeowners [feel] that while their membership is provided for, they as individuals [have] little voice, no one to speak for them within the management business." A successful property manager cannot lose sight of someone as challenging as managing the board and the membership can be.

Professionals who have experience in the field of stress balancing logistics while still catering to individuals and suggest that property managers should split their time between being in the field and being in the office 60/40. He also suggests having an assistant manager at the office to monitor the manager's calls and transfer communications. Like other issues in these Internet immediacy days, it is anticipated that a property manager should act immediately, which translates into the imperative of predicting potential needs.

Expert in Decorum, Staffing and More

As well as looking to the future, a property manager will always be actively present, visiting each building in their portfolio at least once or twice a week — although not on a fixed timetable of visits. Managing the workers of the company means keeping them on their feet, and a consistent visiting schedule helps discourage a facility from slipping into disarray during the times when the staff realize that there will be no management pop-ins.

The manager has to provide support to building superiors and staff, according to Gold. However, if a staffing relationship does not work, Gold says, "A super fires himself." It is the job of the manager to help the super, explain what needs to be done, and provide sufficient time to handle things properly. Ultimately a property manager must do what is best for the entire building and community. Whether the manager fires a member of staff, or the member of staff fires themselves, is a matter of perspective with the same end result.

A good manager must also act professionally when dealing with professionals associated with the running of a building, such as attorneys, accountants, or other service providers. Dealing with lawyers and accountants requires the same basic interpersonal and communication skills that are needed to work with anyone, with an understanding of exactly what duties a professional must perform.

In terms of accountants, an structured property manager makes the role of the accountant simpler by keeping the building funds in order and by providing the board of directors with the financial statement on a monthly rather than annual basis. Maybe the accountant comes for a tax season audit in April, once a year. If the manager has kept up with the paperwork and delivered it to the board, the materials required will already be thorough and properly organized.

In the other hand, the lawyers' duties include raising arrears, and enforcing the decisions of the council. The managing agent is best prepared to support lawyers in carrying out their practice by attending each board meeting.

Whether checking a boiler, reminding the board of a new rule, or simply ensuring that the board of directors has all the appropriate materials on a monthly basis (especially in case a new manager or management firm takes over), the role of a good property manager is never finished. If you have someone who can test the oil or gas rates against the schedule, console a client with a sick cat, and mediate a dispute between two members of staff, chances are you have a keeper.

A effective property manager must be able to collaborate and connect with a number of various persons and cultures while keeping in order all logistics. It is a tough job keeping the engine of a building running 24 hours a day, seven days a week. So, just let him or her know if your manager is a keeper.

Other duties may include as stated above.
Seeking New Locators
Property manager responsibilities normally encompass tenant management. That's the primary responsibility of the landlords and there is plenty that can outsource it to property managers. The tenant management is often involved in locating and attracting tenants. Residential property owners must step in on the empty rental units of the property. The selling of a rented house is also a part of the job description. They will need to market the rentals and add to the associated listing pages and other rental advertising sites convincing advertisements.
Screening inmates
Property manager responsibilities also include ensuring new prospective tenants are trusted. Here, professional property managers often have a special tenant screening process which goes

through the credit history and prospective tenant backgrounds. The good news here is that the more and faster they can choose the right tenants to prevent daily apartment shortages, the more people they watch over time.

Catching tenants: It is the duty of the property owners to fill vacancies. They'll advertise the deposit, and make an ad that's compelling. They also understand what is attracting renters to help build the house, and they can provide tips.

Screening Applicants: Property managers will have a robust screening process that includes regular credit inspections and criminal record checks which can minimize incentives for the tenant's turnover. Experienced property managers have seen hundreds, even thousands of tenants so they have a better idea of how to select the right tenants; those who will pay their rent on time have a longer tenancy and less trouble creating.

Handling Leases: This would include determining the length of the deal and ensuring that all the clauses necessary to protect the landlord are included there. That includes determining the amount required to make the security deposit.

Handling Complaints / Emergencies: The property manager may handle maintenance, noise and emergency requests.

Handling Move Outs: When a tenant moves out, the manager is responsible for inspecting the unit, checking for damages and determining which portion of the security deposit will be returned to the tenant. When they move out, they are responsible for cleaning the building, repairing any damage and finding a new tenant.

Dealing with Evictions: If a homeowner refuses to pay rent or breaches the terms of a contract otherwise, the property manager must understand and act with the correct way of filing an expulsion.

Securing Ownership

The property manager's duties at the holiday home also go beyond routine maintenance. They will also either have to employ security guards or install adequate monitoring devices, or both, to secure their home. Its role will also include establishing emergency preparedness policies and procedures. The more comfortable the tenants have the more secure the property is, that is something a competent property manager is sure of. That will improve customer satisfaction.

Building maintenance

The property management obligations also include land maintenance. This will ensure that the house is in excellent shape as well as offering residents a secure place. Maintenance means investigating and resolving complaints by tenants, and enforcing occupancy rules. They will also check and restore and refurbish all vacant buildings, or handle the jobs of contractors where necessary. Note that even basic maintenance at colder locations can include contracting snow removal services.

Rent, set up, and adjustment

Rent compilation is a basic obligation for every estate owner. Therefore, since this task is gladly outsourced by landlords to property managers, property manager responsibilities may also include the management of leases. The property manager will generally also define and set up the rent collection systems for the tenants. They would also need to have stringent late payment terms and fines, and use a system to verify all rentals as negotiated. In addition;

Setting Rent: The property manager would set the level of lease appropriate to attract tenants to your property. To determine the rent price, the property manager must examine the market where the property is located, and compare comparable properties in the area.

Collecting Rent: The property manager develops a tenant lease collection system. They are setting a monthly rent collection date and strictly enforcing late fees to ensure an optimal cash flow.

Rent adjustment: The property manager can raise the rent annually, in accordance with specific state and/or local law. They'll only lower the rent when they feel it's necessary.

The property manager is also usually responsible for determining a rental rate, in addition to receiving the rents. To compete effectively they need to learn this. A property manager must adjust the rents in order to attract tenants but also to generate rental income for the owners. Depending on the developments in the real estate market, the property manager may also increase or decrease the annual rent.

The real estate managers' responsibilities include coordinating the locator turnover. Home owners are usually the ones that are expected to prepare to move in and out as humans. The property owners will have to look for vandalism in the rental spaces after former tenants, schedule maintenance and repair any breaches before new tenants move in.

In certain cases the property management manages the evictions where the tenants are having issues. That means they should be familiar with the landlord-tenant rules and have the confidence to be comfortable in coping with the case.

Maintenance and handling of complaints are likewise common property management responsibilities. For example, if someone has frequent parties at the property and the neighbors complain about it, it is likely that the property manager is the one to deal with it. Sometimes property managers even have to deal with emergency situations so you should also be aware of the security precautions for the property.

Professional property managers need to have in-depth knowledge of relevant owner tenancy legislation regarding screening applicants, security deposit management, termination of contracts and evictions, as well as complying with property protection requirements. They should obey this and all the rules set out in the lease agreements. This may also entail challenging potential infringers.

Occasionally, the roles and role of a property manager may well be much more than one which meets the eye. Yeah, property managers' duties do include the more obvious everyday errands and utilities, but they should also run the entire show in the background. That is when the real estate investor wants to use the full spectrum of available support for property management out there. Property managers may be asked to perform all analysis, planning, and management of the property. To this end, they need a wide array of expertise and experience in real estate management.

TYPES OF PROPERTIES

Real estate can be defined as the land with all the improvements created to that land by human activity, e.g. homes, buildings, farms, ranches etc. It also includes natural resources such as minerals, fruit, and real estate. These improvements involving human activity, such as water pipes or sewer pipes and above the ground fence, landscaping, buildings, etc., may be below ground.
Real estate can also be synonymous with real estate, but can also be defined as the rights attached to the land, in that real estate has advantages and interests in property ownership.

Land can be defined as the surface of the earth downward to the center of the earth, and infinitely upward. It contains all that's attached to it, namely trees and water. Ice rights, surface rights and subsurface rights (minerals and natural resources, such as gold, coal, shale, oil, etc.) are also found in property.

For the real estate investor, immovable property is much more than a house or plot. Legally it can be described with different terms but the definition is universal. Real estate developers need to grasp the legal terms applicable to real estate, property assets, and land. The term real estate comes from the term real estate, meaning land and all that is permanently attached to it for centuries.

Let us discuss forms of properties from a broader perspective;

AGRICULTURE
Immovable property types include agriculture. Agriculture uses the field to supply food, to grow plants and animals (trees, orchards, etc.). These types of investments may deliver a varied portfolio that contains much of the same real estate investment benefits. The owner has the option of purchasing, selling and leasing farm land. The investor can also invest, for example, in the actual farming business itself, buying a farm or ranch that produces beef cattle while the farmer or rancher manages the operation.

Subsistence Farming – This farming can be either primitive or intensive, which is done for farm owners' consumption. The main goal here is to fulfill the needs of the farmer and his kin.

Primitive subsistence farming is the type of subsistence farming typically done with traditional tools such as hoe, dao, digging sticks etc. on small areas of land. Rather this is the most natural method of growing crops, because the natural environment such as heat, rain, wind and soil condition contribute to crop growth. Furthermore, primitive agriculture includes:

- *Shifting cultivation: Farmers clear the cultivated land in this primitive method, after harvesting the crops and burning the land. As a result, they maintain the soil's fertility, so anyone using next land can get a good yield. This method is known in different regions of India, by different names.*
- *Nomadic herding: This type of method of farming involves herders and farmers who travel from place to place with their animal flocks. And, the herders also provide the livestock with fur, milk, skin, and dairy products.*

Commercial Agriculture
It is commercial farming, as farmers cultivate crops and rear animals for economic development. Farmers develop greater fields of land, with heavy use of machines, due to the need for a high volume of production.

Commercial Agriculture has three main categories:

Commercial grain farming – Just as the name implies, farmers cultivate grain in this process and sell it on the market. Wheat and maize are the most common commercial grain cultivation crops. Asian farmers, Europe, North American temperate grasslands generally practice this type of agriculture.

- *Planting – Planting is a mixture of agriculture and industry, and is practiced across a vast area of land. Plant owners typically cultivate a single crop in a plantation, such as banana, coffee, tea, etc., and use technical assistance to produce the crop on the farm itself or a factory attached to it. The final result also works to industry as a raw material. The rubber industry, for example, uses as raw material the rubber produced from their plantation.*
- *Mixed farming – This method of farming involves growing crops, rearing livestock and growing their forage. Mixed farming for a living is a common practice in parts of the USA, Australia and New Zealand, Europe and South Africa.*

Types of Agricultural Properties

Farms
A Farm is an area of land primarily devoted to agricultural uses, producing food, plants, and cattle-raising.

Ranching

A ranch resembles a farm, and can be a synonym. The main difference, however, is that a farm produces food and other crops, and a ranch serves the purpose of raising grazing livestock, for example cattle, sheep, etc.

Timberland

Timberland is an immovable property covered by forest suitable for timber. There are several ways in which an investor can invest in timberland, such as timber exchange traded funds or ETFs, and REITs or real estate investment trusts containing products related to timberland. And the investor can buy timber-related land and sell the timber out.

Orchards

An orchard is real estate that contains planting fruit trees, such as apples, oranges, grapes, etc.

RESIDENTIAL

Another type of real estate will of course include homes. These residential properties are specifically designed to address multi-family and single-family housing in urban, suburban and rural areas as well. People are driven through the residential category to buy real property, in that many strive for homeownership.

Home Ownership

Homeownership brings financial stability to many, and many believe it is an asset which includes long-term investment. According to Robert

Kiyosaki and his Rich Dad Poor Dad series, however, he advocates a home being just an asset if it puts money in your pocket and it's a liability when all it does is take money out of your pocket. In other words, your house is not an asset, it is a liability, unless you have adequate real estate cash flow.

Although, the principles of Robert Kiyosaki in the financial literacy perspective are fundamental life-altering. It doesn't prevent a lot of people from wanting and longing for homeownership even when it's a responsibility. Homeownership benefits and disadvantages exist, but whatever choice you make, be sure that if any debt is taken out, learn how the mortgage industry works and study how you can use a HELOC to pay off the house faster, thereby saving thousands and hundreds of thousands of thousands of interests through speed banking.

Residential property Types

Homes for single families
Detached or attached homes may include single-family homes, e.g. townhouses. Perhaps single-family homes are the most commonly used and most common forms of real-estate housing.

Apartment Buildings
Apartment buildings or multifamily units enable many crowded areas to get people's housing. Usually those buildings are located in urban areas and suburban areas. In a rural area, it would be

rare to see anything resembling an apartment building. Safety, gym, laundromat, parking, swimming pool, health center and often a golf course can also be accessed in these buildings. Many investors love the multifamily units because of their risk limitations, lack of competition, and ease of administration. But for such types of real estate investments, a greater level of capital is usually required.

Condominium

Except in terms of ownership the condominium is the same as an apartment building. Where one business or proprietor owns an apartment building. Condos can be privately owned. These condominiums will have a homeownership association (HOA) or management, which will be responsible for the building's general maintenance. The condominiums are similar to apartment buildings, sharing common features such as elevators, security system, swimming pool, tennis court, and other amenities.

Cooperative

A cooperative is a unique type of home ownership, in that you become a shareholder in a corporation that owns the real estate when an investor purchases into a property. Growing shareholder shall have the right to possess one unit of residence per shareholder agreement. It is a pooling of cooperative members who gain their advantages in the purchasing power by reducing the cost of member services and maintenance.

Manufactured homes
Manufactured homes are built entirely from the factory, delivered to the site, and installed. These homes are constructed under the supervision and administered by the United States. Housing and Urban Development Department (HUD); Those forms of homes were known as mobile homes until June 15, 1976. These homes can be relatively low cost due to its assembly-line-type construction from its factories and the newer modern styles with space are making these types of homes more attractive to buyers.

COMMERCIAL PROPERTIES
Commercial estates are another type of real estate. Business properties may include infrastructure that includes commercial operations, such as office buildings, shopping complexes, parks, restaurants, and entertainment venues. Many examples of commercial properties are the restaurants, motels, and also parking facilities. It also Comprises shopping malls and centers, medical and educational buildings, hotels and offices. Includes non-residential structures such as office buildings, warehouses, and retail structures as well. These buildings can be either standalone or in train stations. Apartment buildings, though used for residential purposes, are also called institutional. It is because they are owned for producing income. Commercial buildings include office buildings, warehouses, and retail buildings (e.g. convenience stores, 'big box'

shops, and shopping malls). A commercial building may combine functions with retailing on the floor. If space allocated to multiple functions is significant these buildings can be called multi-use.

Let us see some types that we have.

Business properties
Company properties can include any real estate owned by a corporate body. More importantly, business property can refer to real business residences and activity. For example, a mechanic shop with a garage is called commercial property.

Office Services
Office room is a property which has an area where the business operation can take place. Regus, a company that rents office space on a full-time commitment to small businesses or to people who don't need to rent office space. Some companies provide usage-based leasing and provides many office space areas including conference spaces,

Shopping malls
Shopping malls are real estate, concerned primarily with shopping. Many buyers opt for REITs which are investments in shopping malls / centers.

Shops

The shopping market is also another business field that can broaden a portfolio of buyers.

Theatres
Entertainment, such as movie complexes and theatres. This is yet another potential strategy ignored by buyers.

Hotels
Hotels are great real estate and many real estate investors, as they eventually invest in the hotel business once they expand their portfolio of properties.

Parking spaces
Parking lots are another alternative, and overlooked type of real estate. Such parking lots and facilities will easily switch on autopilot, that is, very little maintenance, through artificial intelligence (AI) and emerging technology (e.g. apps).

INDUSTRIAL
Industrial is another form of real estate that acquires such buildings as warehouses, power plants, and factories. The industrial sector is the least talked about and concentrated real estate for many developers to invest in. Yet investing in commercial real estate shouldn't be ignored for the developer. Industrial real estate is an umbrella term for fabrication, manufacturing, research and development, storage and distribution. While industrial property is often overshadowed

by glitzier sectors such as residential, commercial and retail, industrial property should not be ignored as an integral enabler of global trade and as a robust, revenue-generating asset class.

Industrial Real property makes the global economy boom. Well-located, high-quality industrial real estate keeps the supply chains around the world running, allows for trade and e-commerce, and ensures the efficient flow of goods from producers to markets.

The industrial real estate industry covers properties used by firms during the course of a business operation. These properties include offices, warehouses, garages, and distribution centers as examples. Industrial properties can provide docking bays in which trucks are able to load and unload items.

Types of industrial properties

Warehouses
A warehouse is a facility used for stockpiling goods and resources. Yet, these factories don't just stack the goods and keep them there for a long time. Many warehouses are active, in that wholesalers, importers, exporters and so on all use warehouses to keep products and goods flowing to their customers. An customer will take note of future warehouse investment prospects.

Factories

Additionally, factories may be classified as a manufacturing plant and consist of houses, machines, and equipment where products are manufactured in a complex systemic process. At a side line, factories started after the industrial revolution, when other goods were unable to keep up with the production and demand from small workshops. Factories, however, are yet another neglected investment. The biggest investments sometimes are those the fly under the radar because people are not looking for it.

Energy stations

Electric stations or steam stations provide our energy and generate our energy. With the rise and the greener and greener technology drive. Innovation has given us the opportunity to make some fascinating and potentially groundbreaking investments.

Other properties may include;

Mixed-utility

Mixed-use property is an immovable property category which has several uses for that property. That is commercial and residential within the same house, for example.

Special purpose

Special purpose property is a type of real property generally held by the public, e.g. places of religion, schools, libraries, government buildings, cemeteries, and parks.

Investors, in particular, have multiple sectors to choose how to grow their investment portfolio in the real estate field. This article shows the six categories of real estate, namely agricultural, residential, business, manufacturing, mixed-use and special use. There is an investing market, of innovation and analysis, for just about everyone of their taste.

PREPARATION OF PROPERTIES

Real estate brokers are able to reassure you that a house that has been properly prepared to be sold will still sell quicker than a house that has not been ready to be sold, and for more money. This is why, should you want to start a real estate listing-preparation program, real estate agents can become the number one source of referral. Cracked windows, peeling paint and rotting porch boards all leave a lasting impression with the wrong impression from potential homebuyers! When you see a rundown car you immediately believe it will run like junk as well. Homes are like peeling paint which immediately evokes the feeling that the wood behind it needs to be rotted. Using your handyperson skills, you can do small maintenance, fix what needs to be done, and basically give your customer's homes a general spruce-up before selling. It's not unusual for the retailer to be compensated by getting their money back several times before they sell, since technical and aesthetic defects often add up to a lower agreed sale price.

PROPERTY COST ANALYSIS

Evaluation of properties, assessment of real estate, assessment of properties or assessment of land is the method of forming a value judgment, for real property (usually market value). Real estate transactions also require evaluations because they arise infrequently and each property is unique (especially its condition, a key valuation factor), unlike company securities that are traded on a regular basis and are similar. The place also plays a crucial valuation function. Since property can't change location, however, it's often the home upgrades or improvements that can change its value. Assessment reports form the basis for mortgage loans, divorce and estate settlements, taxation, and so on. An appraisal report is often used to determine a sale price for a house.

Price versus value: There might be variations between what the land actually is worth (market value) and what it costs (price) to purchase it. A price paid may not represent market value for that property. Perhaps there may have been special circumstances, such as a special

arrangement between buyer and seller over which one party has control or substantial power on the other party. The sale may have been in other cases only one of many assets owned or shared by two parties. In such cases, the price paid for any particular piece is not its "value" market (with the idea usually being that all the pieces and prices add up to the market value of all the pieces) but its "price" market.

At other times, if his subjective valuation of the property (his investment value for him) was higher than the market value, a buyer may willingly pay a premium price above the generally accepted market value. One particular example of this is a rival land owner who may achieve economies of scale and added value (plotting value) by integrating his own land with the subject property (assemblage). Similar situations occasionally occur in corporate finance. This may arise, for example, when a merger or takeover happens at a price that is greater than the value indicated by the underlying stock price. The standard reason for these kinds of mergers and acquisitions is that "the total is greater than its parts," because a company's overall ownership grants it complete control. Sometimes this is something that buyers will pay a high price for. This condition can also arise in sales of immovables.

Knowing the value of your property

Whether you plan to sell your home in private, or just challenge your local estate agent 's opinion, here's all you need to know about valuing your own home.

After all said and done now, how do you then value your property? How do you know the value of your property? Let us highlight some ideas.

Know how much identical properties are being sold for

Were you aware that you can now check property selling prices across the UK? Zoopla – for instance – uses data from the Land Registry to show how many homes sell for on a given street or town. The appearance of newly sold properties may take a few months, but Zoopla's tool allows you to search property prices from as far back as 1995. Also if you aren't in the business of valuing your own home, taking a gander at the local housing market can be very interesting!

Understanding the emerging real estate market

For get a high-level understanding of the current property market, you could do worse than checking out The Land Registry 's UK House Price Index which shows recent sales prices in your local area as well as nationally. Real rates can still be listed, including the estimated sales price for property in the UK and the general condition of the new Halifax housing market.

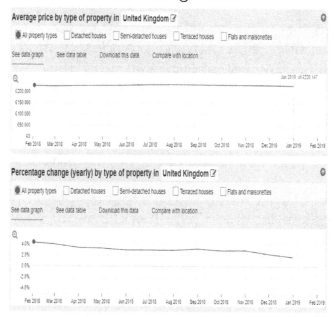

Look at home business predictions

While none (not even us!) can fully predict what will happen to UK housing market, some websites offer predictions based on both market growth rate and economic climate.

Use the Tools online

Many websites provide resources to help you enjoy your house. Zoopla can offer you, for example, an approximation of what your home might be worth based on the recent selling prices in your local area. Alternatively, you can choose a specific street home to gain a tailor-made valuation based on the current real estate market as well as previous property selling prices.

Based on the upper and lower ranges for your land, Property Price Advice provides a more detailed review elsewhere. You can also try Mouseprice, although it tends to provide much rougher estimates since it only requires your home 's number or bedrooms and your postcode.

Check the previous selling price for your property

The value of your home can be found based on its previous selling price. When you bought your home, Nationwide's House Price Calculator takes into account what it could be worth right now. This tool does not take any home improvements that you may have made since you purchased your property into consideration however.

Take your local area into consideration

The positioning of your house has a huge effect on your home 's valuation. The possibility of rain, for example, may have a major effect on the sale price. Also, checking this when you buy a new home is imperative, as it could save you thousands of pounds. The Environment Authority has extensive details on areas at risk of floods as well as sources of air pollution such as landfill sites.

Home-check is a website that lets you assess the total flood and subsidence effect. You'll be able to figure out how vulnerable your home is to other environmental variables by testing your postcode. You can also check that your area has landfill waste

It's always best to test the crime rate in your immediate area because that will impact the price of your transaction. Potential buyers would search for homes with low crime rates, especially those with children. You can check the rates of local crime by searching for Police.uk which provides information on each street about recorded crimes.

This is important to determine the valuation of real estate for a number of purposes, including finance, sales listing, profit research, land insurance and taxes. But for most individuals, the most important method of real estate valuation is deciding the selling or purchasing price of a piece of real estate. This article will include an introduction to the basic principles and methods of valuing immovable property, particularly when it relates to sales. Valuing property is hard because each property has specific features such as venue, lot size, floor plan and amenities. Concepts of the general real estate market such as supply and demand in a given region will surely play into the overall value of a particular property. However, particular property must be subject to valuation to determine a reasonable value, using one of several approaches.

Basic Valuation Concepts.

In technical terms, the value of a property is defined as the present value of future benefits arising from the property's ownership. Unlike other quick-use consumer products, real-estate advantages are typically recognized over a long period of time. An estimation of the value of a property must also take into account economic and social patterns, as well as regulatory restrictions or legislation and environmental factors which can affect the four value elements:

- Demand: ownership desire or need supported by the financial means to satisfy the desire
- Utility: The opportunity to fulfill the wants and desires of prospective owners
- Scarcity: Finite provision of competing properties
- Transferability: The ease of transfer of property rights

Market Value
An assessment is an opinion or estimate of the value of a given property as of a specific date. In making choices on real estate deals, appraisal reports are used by corporations, government departments, entities, creditors and mortgage firms. The aim of an assessment is to determine

the market value of a property – the most likely price the property will bring into a competitive and open market. The selling price will not necessarily reflect the real value, the price at which the property eventually sells. For example, if a seller is under duress due to the threat of foreclosure, or if it holds a private sale, the property may sell below its market value.

AROUSING CLIENT INTEREST IN PROPERTY

How do you make your client feel that if he or she doesn't purchase that property, he or she is missing out? This might not be a big deal from the sound of it, nut being able to get into the mind of your buyer and convince their thoughts about your products or property is a rick and very important skill-set in this field.

A customer support team that works consistently generates a good brand identity and develops high customer loyalty. Moreover, customers might be able to call you with questions about your offers. All communications relating to grievances, questions or even feedback from customers should be handled in this manner, so that they end up in sales. Here are some basics highlighted below;

Be natural and do not use scripts.

Customers want to phone because they want to have a chat with a live human that can answer their concerns, including the odd questions.

If it were otherwise, customers would continue browsing the website. For this reason the ready-made conversation scripts should never be used. These kinds of pre-written responses sound strange to the consumer and generate a sense of an unwelcome sales process. If you develop an intimate relationship with a vendor, consumers are more likely to purchase.

It would not be possible to create such ties if the consultant reads the previously planned discussion scenario aloud. So if you wonder how to persuade the customer to purchase your product, do one thing-be natural and act like a human being.

Close to 60 percent of consumers choose to contact small companies whether they have, or are interested in, questions or complaints about their product. When a customer wants to get details fairly easily and enjoys personal touch, phone calls always win. Because of this, you should never use or impose ready-made conversation scenarios, so-called scripts, on your sales reps. Sales scripts should be used in an ideal world to guide the conversation and help the representative of your company address the most important issues, or suggest words that encourage buying.

Scripts can by no way be viewed as rigid situations to which any salesperson will stick. Of all, even the actors improvise and their interpretations always turn out to be different than what the scriptwriter had expected.

The comments read from a sheet of paper or from a computer screen sound false and raise the doubt of a prospective customer right away. Immediately the buyer begins to think that the sole purpose of a salesperson is to sell a product no matter what.

People are more likely to buy a rep to establish partnerships, and seek to communicate with them. That kind of bond would not be feasible if the salesperson reads from a pre-written outline and hates going through the scheme. How can one persuade someone to buy something? Do not act like a robot!

Ask about the clients' well-being.

Ask the customer about his / her wellbeing at the start of the conversation while introducing yourself.

Research has revealed that sales within the group of customers, who were asked about their well-being, are increasing significantly. On a positive note you can also initiate a conversation.

A waiter's experiment showed that positive comments raised the tip by 27 per cent! It works well during the discussion over the phone.

Use names while talking with a client.

Figure out the name of your customer, and use it from time to time. Psychological research shows that when the other side uses it, people like to hear their name and are much more likely to make a friendly relation.

Pay attention to proper forms whilst having a conversation in Polish. You can address the client by name in English without being afraid to commit a faux pas. It is not easy in Polish though.

So ask them if they agree, before you start addressing the client. You'll avoid awkwardness with that technique.

If you don't want to annoy the customer, using the "Mr. / Miss" phrase. How to encourage customers to buy your product-a rather obvious example-treat them as people, not as leads listed in a CRM system you are using.
Prove that your products are better than those offered by competitors.

Keep initiating further conversation.

Lead and initiate a conversation, ask open questions and offer an opportunity for the interlocutor to develop the topic.
If you don't know how to persuade a customer, try this: instead of saying: "So our product has this function," say: "Yes, (customer's name), our

product has such a function, and I'm happy to tell you how it works."

Prove that your products are better than those offered by competitors

It's really important to show the value of a product or service that the company provides.

Often, customers call businesses to ask questions about the product for market research. Therefore, if you have an opportunity, emphasize that your offer is better (because it gives access to some special functions, it allows customization, it is technically superior) and/or cheaper than the competitor (it is worth using specific values here, e.g. at 20 per cent).

If the offer isn't cheaper – it's more difficult, but you can always mention that the customer receives a better product for a slightly higher price.

Specify the positive characteristics of the customer.

Psychologists have proven that if we mention the positive aspects of some clients during the conversation, they will try to act accordingly in our attitude towards them.
How does that have an impact on incoming calls and phone sales?
Try to emphasize the importance of one when you talk to the client, by saying: "You are one of

our best clients" or "It's a pleasure to do business with you."

You are encouraging the client to be the best customer in this way!

Act on emotions.

We all like to think that our decisions are rational, but let's face it-most of them influence our emotions.

Stress what emotional feelings the company or its buying would induce while talking to a customer. You will see it functions more successfully than having an factual statement!

Present yourself as a business representative, consultant or advisor.

Just to clarify-we don't recommend you pose yourself as a business consultant if you don't operate as one, or deceive and lie about your position. However, there is a huge difference between acting like a professional who represents a company and behaving like a typical, pushy sales representative.

Don't be the seller who has a walking list of goods or services in mind. Don't be the salesperson who recites in stock a list of products and doesn't care about what their client wants. Then this kind of a selling pep just talks about whether to persuade the buyer to purchase your stuff-evidence of this can be found somewhere in other papers on

"How to persuade someone to purchase it"-bad

practices.

Think of yourself as an experienced person with a lot of knowledge. After all, you have industry experience that you represent, you have a general overview of your sector, while consumers know only a slice of that. Use your hard-earned knowledge to present your recommendations and provide your customers with new information.

And it's not just about trying to play for a sales talk. When you realize how much experience you have and start more than ever believing in yourself, your voice will sound more confident and give more persuasive power to your words.

You no longer need to talk about how to get people to purchase a commodity, just using your expertise.

Leverage FOMO

Particularly undecided buyers always find resigning from a great opportunity challenging-especially if they are aware of what they would sacrifice by giving it up. This phenomenon is named FOMO (Fear of Missing Out Fear) in marketing. That term means a fear of losing the chance to buy / do something. In situations where you really don't know how to encourage a customer to buy your product, you can use this psychological trick-an example of this could be as follows:

present your offer as something that a potential customer will miss if they don't make a purchase, instead of simply emphasizing the added value of the product.

A good example would also be to think about how to persuade a client to cooperate with an agency for the real estate. You may say that the offer is time-limited, that your company later does not envisage this type of cooperation, and that the apartment or office space will no longer be available, because its owner is considering seeking buyers abroad.

To find a sweet spot on how to persuade a buyer to purchase your company (in this case: an apartment or office room that you're offering), you can always say that it's an odd occurrence for such a high quality of real estate to be available on the market.

Adjust your offer as far as possible to describe a potentially lost opportunity from every possible perspective. What's missing in a client's life or business without this solution right now? Why are they not going to regret doing a purchase? How do your competitors use this if they reject your offer?

Let your customers decide on the next steps.

If you want to know how to persuade someone to buy your product, please follow our last tip. Using the strength of psychology in your job to offer more flexibility to your future customer by asking: "What would you want to do next?" or "What next steps will we take? "It's going to help you sound less like a salesman and more like a consultant. It's one of the most important steps to persuade people to buy your product.

Of course, you can recommend any solutions to pick from or any suggestions of the next steps. But, by posing this kind of problem and encouraging the client to decide for himself, without pressuring or persuading any of the choices, you give a signal to the person you are talking to that their input matters.

What is the legal interest in a real estate?

The legal interest in a real estate refers to the right to own or use property. It belongs to the lawful owner, who is the person recorded on the title deeds at the Land Registry. Legal interest gives the owner the right to control the property, which means they can decide to sell the property or to transfer it.

What is the beneficial interest in a real estate?

The beneficial interest represents an interest in a property's economic benefit. It belongs to the beneficial owner, who is entitled to the land's financial value, irrespective of Land Registry title entries.

- Beneficial interests in particular give right to:
- Live in real estate;
- A share of the profits from rents;
- A share of the sale proceeds, if the property is sold.

The legal owner and the beneficial landowner may be the same person but not necessarily the same person. In fact, when two parties agree to control property in a trust, legitimate ownership and beneficial possession would be separated: the legitimate owner - whose identity is registered at the Land Registry - owns the property 'on trust' for the benefit of someone else, the beneficial owner. We claim the "bar manager" is the legitimate owner, while the beneficial owner is the "beneficiary."

Other ways of reaching out to your potential investor or customer are listed below;

- Advertise on Google with Google Ads
- Make Quality Videos
- Use Social Media like a Pro
- Start a Real Estate Blog
- Take Advantage of Real Estate Services and Websites
- Create Newsletters

RENT COLLECTION

Establishing a method for collecting rent on a monthly basis will make it easier to keep track of which tenants are current with their rent and which ones are behind on rent. Each estate owner must decide which option works best for their particular situation. There are various ways to reach out to your customer and request for rent payment, there are also various means and pre-arranged procedures to follow this up. Before you decide on the method you would want to employ to request for rent, you need some basic backup information from the client. The aim of this is to make collation and monitoring on the long run easier. Some of these are highlighted below;

1. Tenants / Rental Units Number:

If you have 20 rental units of your own, you probably don't want to knock on 20 doors personally to collect the rent on the first of each month. You'll want a more efficient and streamlined way of collecting rent.

2. Rent Property Distance:

If you live away from your rentals, it may be better for you to hire a third party to collect the rent or to do an electronic transfer of funds.

3. Desire to interact with your tenants:

You may have only two rental units, and may live less than a mile from your rental property, but you prefer to have a more hands-off management approach. In this case, a deposit from electronic funds or the mail may be the best way to get your rent.

4. How comfortable with Technology you are:

You may prefer to collect the rent in person if you are not comfortable with the technology.

There are several different ways your tenants can collect rent. These methods include collecting the rent personally, and outsourcing the collection of rent to a third party. Below are five possibly worth considering options. When deciding on a method of rent collection, you have to include a clause in the lease agreement that clearly explains the rent collection procedure

Rent Collection Online:
One way is online to accept the rental payments. If the primary method you use to collect rental

payments is online, you generally have to allow another form of payment for those who do not have access to online resources, such as paying rent by mail.

There are many online sites that offer landlords on-line payment services. These sites include ERentPayment, RentMatic, RentMerchant and others. To find the place that best suits your needs you should do a search for online rental collection services.

Prices will vary according to selected plan. Some platforms or plans are very simplistic in that the only service provided is simple rent collection. Other sites may have more bells and whistles with services that might include an online rental roll, the ability to upload important forms and documents for your tenants and the ability to send messages to your tenants.

Pay by Mail picks up:
You should opt to give tenants their rental payments by fax. This saves you time collecting the payments yourself.

There are certain issues to this method. The envelope may, for example, be postmarked by the appropriate date, but you might not collect the payment until a few days later. Technically, the deposit wouldn't be deemed late, but you'd still not have it on schedule. Additionally, if the tenant pays their rent only partially, sending it in the mail will buy them a few extra days until you find out.

Allowing the mail payment method also allows the age-old excuse of "the check got lost in the mail." To prevent this, your tenant can obtain a mailing certificate from the post office which costs a little more than a dollar. This certificate serves as evidence that the mail was sent when the landlord says it was. It does not however verify the actual amount in the envelope.

Drop-Off position:

If you have an office at this location for your property investing business, you may choose to allow tenants to drop off the rent. I would not recommend that your tenants be allowed to drop off payments at your home address or give your home address to your tenants, unless, of course, you live at the same address as your tenant. Be careful not to leave out cash-filled envelopes that can be stolen or a resident can say that they left a certain amount but you find less in the envelope.

Rent in Person Collection:

You can decide to collect rental payments from all tenants individually. The good part about that is that you'll immediately have the payment in your hands. The worst news is that having to schedule delivery times for all of the tenants is time-consuming and stressful. However, sometimes this is the best method if you are paid rent in cash, since you can carefully count all the money by hand and give them a receipt of the transaction.

Enterprise Property Management:
Finally, by hiring a property management company, you could opt to completely outsource rent collection to a third party. Not only can this company collect rent payments for you, but all tenant complaints can also be handled, maintenance issues handled and vacancies filled in. You'll be asked to sign a contract with the company and pay an negotiated price depending on the services you order.

INVESTMENT PROTECTION

Scope and definition of "investment": Investment is typically different from trade in goods and services, which is covered by other treaties. "Foreign investment involves the transfer of tangible or intangible assets from one country to another for the purpose of using them to generate wealth in that country; under full or partial control of the owner of those assets."

Can the mere participation in a tender in another country be treated as a "investment" and covered by a BIT, though? How about hopes of benefit, or risk assumption? The trend in BITs has been to expand the definition of foreign investment to include more than just branch setting up. However, each BIT sets out different guidelines and those issues need to be resolved on a case-by - case basis.

Investment protection is a broad economic term that refers to any form of guarantee or insurance that investments made are not going to be lost, which can be due to fraud or anything else. For example, the Investment Protection Bureau is a New York state legal body charged under the New York State Securities Law (the Martin Act) with monitoring and limiting investment to protect the public from fraud. Most other protection is of this form, monitoring and legally preventing brokers and comparable individuals from misusing investment.

Unlike what happens in the goods and services trade, there is no single multilateral investment protection agreement. Conversely, States have entered into bilateral or multilateral investment treaties (BITs or MITs) protecting individuals or businesses from one country investing in another. While the text of these treaties differs, it has been the practice of government to include similar standards in all the agreements. The website of the United Nations Conference on Trade and Development (UNCTAD) defines Bilateral Investment Treaties as "agreements between two countries for mutual encouragement, promotion and protection of investment in each other's territories by companies based in each country." The organization provides a comprehensive search engine on this website to retrieve existing agreements.

What kind of security does an investment get?

There are essentially four frameworks for protecting investors proposed by States:

- investment legislation;
- investment contracts;
- bilateral investment treaties; and
- multilateral investment treaties.

A state that pass investment legislation guaranteeing investors receive such care. Such legislation could guarantee tax exemption or provide investors in a given industry sector with a specific tax regime. However, creditors may be worried that some of the guarantees found in the law could be vulnerable to a potential government revocation.

An investor can enter into a host State investment contract. Examples of such contracts in the extractive industries are concession agreements and production sharing contracts under which investors are protected to invest in the exploitation of the natural resources of a state. The investment contract will protect creditors from changes in legislation or policy that adversely impact their interests. However, the effectiveness of these clauses can be variable in the face of government action.

One of the most notable aspects of the foreign direct investment boom has been the growth of investment treaties entered into by host states. Investment treaties may take the form of bilateral investment treaties between two states, or multi-state multilateral investment treaties (BITs or MITs). These treaties, designed to encourage foreign investment, commonly include provisions setting out specific investor protections from the respective states. As the name suggests, MITs allow a number of states to offer those protections, often on a regional basis. Recently, major trade agreements have been negotiated, involving nations that control much of the world's trade. For example, the Trans-Pacific Partnership Comprehensive and Progressive Agreement (CPTPP), one of the largest trade agreements after the North American Free Trade Agreement, and the Transatlantic Trade and Investment Partnership (TTIP) between the EU and the US (though negotiations have not been smooth).

Furthermore some other security privileges and protection procedures available to investors. They include;

Admission and establishment (freedom to invest): International law has traditionally permitted States to decide whether or not to authorize a company to enter foreign investment. Today, however, 'some regional and bilateral treaties provide for the right of entry and investment for nationals of contracting states.' In other words, as a result of those treaties, countries have lost their power to refuse entry into certain investments and companies have gained the right to expand their business in those countries.

National treatment: "International Investment Arbitration" which does not prohibit distinctions between foreigners and nationals by "international common law. In order to compensate for this omission, the national treatment requirement, which is included in the majority of investment protection treaties, has the objective of finally providing a level playing field for foreign investors (at least after they have established themselves in the country). "The idea behind this standard is that states cannot stipulate differences between national and foreign investors unless it is necessary for g When this clause is present in a treaty, investors from one country are entitled to receive the same treatment from the other signatory country of the BIT as local investors.

Most-favored-nation status: use of this concept in investment treaties "requires nationals of Member States parties to the arrangement to make use of the preferential treatment given to third-country citizens by any of the contracting states." In other words, if one of the States which has entered into a BIT or an Inst offers advantages to third-country investors, the corporations of the other countries shall benefit.

Equal and fair treatment: this concept is "vague and subject to various definitions." However, the term has been more precise across multiple arbitral awards and can be interpreted today as meaning a certain degree of certainty and predictability, but it does not mean that investment is assured against future risks. State measures applied to investments must therefore result from an administrative due process and must respect legitimate expectations of the investors.

Compensation in the event of expropriation or damage to the investment: BITs generally prohibit both direct expropriation (forcible appropriation by the State of assets by means of administrative or legislative actions) and indirect expropriation (where the effects of the measure are equivalent to direct expropriation but without formal transfer of title or explicit appropriation). In any case, the State still has the authority to take the measure but it must compensate the investor adequately.

Guarantees relating to the free transfer of funds: Some bilateral investment treaties include provisions that ensure that investors are allowed to withdraw dividends and proceeds from their investments and send them to the country of origin of the investors.

"States have the practice of protecting foreign investment through investment treaties, otherwise referred to as the bilateral investment treaty (BIT); foreign investment protection and promotion treaty; multilateral investment treaty (MAI) in English; bilateral investment treaty in

French; and bilateral investment treaty (TBT); BITs are currently an important source of protection for investments. A BIT is an agreement between two states whose purpose is to promote and protect investments made by investors from the other Contracting State in the territory of one Contracting State (the "host state") while furthering the development of both States. Although not all Parts have the same substance, most of them include, inter alia, clauses related to the identification of investments and investors under treaty security and care requirements and conflict resolution procedures between States or between international investors and States. 1959 saw the signing of the first BIT between Germany and Pakistan. There are actually more than 2.700 BITs in place, agreed not only between industrialized and emerging countries, as was their original purpose, but also between developing countries or established states. Some states have a Model BIT that is used as a basis for negotiating investment treaties. For starters, the following cases can be listed in the last decade: India 2003 Model BIT, Canada 2004 Model BIT, France 2006 Model BIT, Colombia 2007 Model BIT, Norway 2007 Draft Model BIT, Germany 2008 Model BIT, and U.S. 2012 Model BIT. Apart from BITs, there are several national arrangements, trade deals, or free trade agreements, which include a chapter referred to as the protection agreement. For now, despite attempts to adopt an MAI within the Organization for Economic Co-operation and Development, there is no general multilateral agreement for the protection (and promotion) of foreign investment."

https://www.oxfordbibliographies.com/view/document/obo -9780199796953/obo-9780199796953-0084.xml

Downside Protection

Downside protection on an investment occurs when the investor or fund manager uses techniques to avoid a fall in the investment's value. Investors and fund managers share a common goal of avoiding losses and many instruments can be used to achieve this goal. It is very popular to use options or other hedging tool to minimize or mitigate losses in the event of a fall in market value. Downside insurance is meant to have a protective net, once the valuation of an investment continues to decline. Downside protection can be done in a variety of ways but the most common is to use options or other derivatives to limit possible losses over time. Protecting an entire portfolio from losses may be meaningless depending on how much the cost of protection and when the investment is expected to be cashed in.

Understanding defense at the back

Security at the bottom comes in several ways. Downside protection often entails buying an option to hedge a long position. Other methods of protection against setbacks include the use of stop losses or the purchase of assets that are negatively correlated to the assets you try to hedge. The more common forms of downside risk, based on derivatives, are often seen as paying for insurance-a necessary cost for some investment protection. Loading up on uncorrelated assets to diversify the portfolio as a whole is a much more involved process that will impact portfolio asset allocation and risk-reward profile. It is necessary to weigh downside protection costs in time and dollars against the importance of the investment, and when it is expected to be sold.

It is always important to remember, of course, that when stocks go up and down, the price increases and decreases represent only gains and losses on paper. An investor has not lost anything until they sell a share in exchange for giving up the share and accept the low price. Investors may choose to wait a period of low performance, but fund managers seeking protection against the downside are usually more pressed for time. Fund managers can sell from multiple positions in their fund if their screens indicate that they should. Exiting weak positions and going to cash can help create downside protection for the net asset value of the fund (the net asset value (NAV) represents an entity's net value and is calculated as the total asset value of the entity minus the total amount of its liabilities. The NAV, most commonly used in the context of a mutual fund or an exchange-traded fund (ETF), represents the fund's per share / unit price on a particular date or time. NAV is the price at which the funds' shares / units registered with the U.S. If the market begins to fall, the Securities and

Exchange Commission (SEC) will be traded (invested or redeemed).

Sometimes the best protection against downside is to wait for a correction on the market. For those who don't want to wait, buying a put option for a given stock would be an example of downside protection. The put option offers the option owner the right to offer the underlying stock's share at a price decided by the position. If the stock price falls, either the investor can sell the stock at the price listed on the put or sell the put, as it will have increased in value because it is in the money. Either approach limits the exposure to losses and offers protection against downside.

Bert, for instance, holds 100 shares of XYZ stock and is very worried about the declining price of XYZ stock because he wants to sell it early. XYZ stock today trades at $35 / share. Bert can purchase a $32 / share put on the 100 shares of XYZ stock. If XYZ stock price falls below $32 / share, the put will give Bert the ability to sell the stock to the put writer for $32 / share. Bert reduced his losses on XYZ stock and provided insurance against downside.

CHAPTER 4
PROPERTY RENTING AND LEASING

In real property, a lease is a contract for a specific period of time — often 6 or 12 months — after which the contract expires, whereas rent is the payment made under the lease conditions. Real estate leases are also generally referred to as "rental agreements."

In the real estate market, a lease is the contractual arrangement which specifies the terms of a property's usage. That involves what is leased, for how long, and certain stipulations that are decided by all parties (e.g., how pets are permitted on the property).

Rent is the periodic payment to the owner of a property (often called "landlord") for the use of such property, which could be a building, residential space (house, apartment, etc.), commercial space (office, store, warehouse, etc.), or land. In other business cases, rent is the payment or series of payments made to a property owner for the use of that property, such as equipment, vehicles, industrial machinery etc. it is also an arrangement where a contract is provided for the exclusive usage of another's own good, service or land. A gross lease is when the tenant pays a flat rental amount and the landlord pays all regularly incurred property charges for

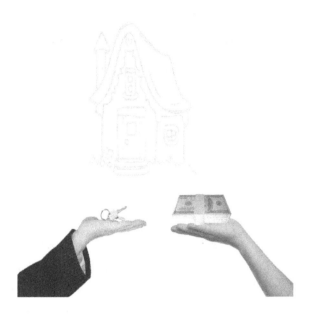

the property. Renting equipment is one example. Renting can be a case in point of sharing economy.

How Long Will a Mortgage last?

Leases are typically scheduled for 6 to 12 months, but can span more or less of the period. The word "rental deal" is a synonym for "leasing."

As a lease is a binding arrangement, all parties are bound to comply by it for the length of the existence. Leasing must be received in a timely and reasonable fashion — typically at 1st of the month — and late fees are also penalized due to the conditions of the contract. In the other side, the land owner cannot, without the consent of the occupant (the rent payer), arbitrarily break the contract or change the conditions. A written agreement to enter a contract (for example, renting a house) is binding in the real estate market. For this purpose, several written proposals should not be made, because more than one may be approved. The person has entered multiple leases at that point, and is required to pay multiple rents.

Lease End

The termination date of a lease requires any party to cancel or renew the conditions for another year (or whichever period the lease defines). In real estate, this is typically performed between 60 to 90 days before the expiration of the leasing contract. This means that renters can notify them that they are leaving, or indicate they are staying. The landlord may indicate that there will be changes, such as an increase in rent (often limited by the lease or by law), which the tenant can either accept, negotiate or deny.

Leasing vs. Month to Month Rent

When a lease expires, tenants are automatically relocated to a "month-to - month" rental agreement unless or until either party signs a new lease with a new expiry date or one or both parties backs out of the month-to - month agreement. In this scenario, tenants generally have to abide by rules laid down in the initial lease, but terms are subject to monthly change.

Month-to - month deals with both landlords and land owners come with big pros and cons. For tenants, month-to - month rental agreements give them the freedom to move whenever they are most convenient, without having to worry about the transfer or breach of a lease agreement. That makes rental income uncertain for property owners. To offset this uncertainty, many property owners choose to charge month-to-month tenants a rent rate that is much higher than those on a lease, a fact that makes month-to-month agreements prohibitive for most tenants. Month to month agreements are more common in some cases and less likely to be related to expired leases. Short-term leases are common in cities with transient populations (e.g. Las Vegas), and are not necessarily associated with higher rent charges.

ADVERTISEMENT AND MARKETING
Real estate marketing is the market of property listings that are purchased and sold through real estate agents or directly to purchasers. In a specific region, such as prices and mortgages, the real estate market sets expectations for properties. In general, the real estate market differs from the property location.

Hot property market: It's essential to buy a property because you're bound to get good deals at an affordable rate. Most home sellers are usually eager to sell house in a hot property to pay by closing deals

Cold real estate market: is not as competitive and prices may exceed expectations
The definition of real estate marketing focuses on offering properties in an area versus demand for houses.
The quantity in a hot real estate market is higher than the real estate buyers, meaning good deals are in stock because agents want to close deals. If you want to buy a home, it is essential that you look at an area 's market to see if there is a high supply.

Setting the market

There are several ways to identify an area with the real estate market. By using inventory the most convenient way to do this is. It may turn out that the inventory is low but you can use it to recognize the state of the market.

The market is not usually consistent with the season, and often varies. You can look at the inventory and determine whether the property buying is a hot season or a cold season.

Whether you're a real estate seller or investor with no idea as to how to go about the real estate business, you should employ an professional real estate agent to gage the bid.

They'll be able to evaluate the market and relay relevant information about when to make a purchase.

Real estate brokers have a great deal of business awareness, and are knowledgeable enough to educate you about what to purchase and what to give. They will also look at prices for sale and listing, and will advise you accordingly.

Basic marketing and advertisement strategies will include;

Adding Property Pages to Social Sharing.
Chances are, home shoppers are happy to share their top housing pics with friends and family, so make it easy for home buyers to email and share different properties online by incorporating social media buttons.

Real estate marketing tips
Keep an eye on the Contest.
What are other realtors in your area doing? What are their websites? How involved are they on social media? Note what is being achieved by competitors – then avoid their mistakes and repeat their performance!

Make Communicating Yourself quick.
Place your contact details on every page of your website. Ideally, you should make an amazing touch with us page that catches attention.

Create a Killer Business Card.

Get a cool looking business card and hand it out on a Friday night like pizza flyers.

Make Use of Local Images.
You 're not selling just a house in many ways, you 're selling a whole town or city. Showcase the best that your area has to offer, with beautiful pictures of local town landmarks and familiar sites of high quality.

Hire a Pro-Photo.
Successful real estate is strongly dependent on great photography. Bad pictures will decrease interest in even the greatest properties. It's absolutely important you have beautiful pictures of your assets. Hire a skilled photographer (preferably with expertise in photographing homes and architecture), or, if you have advanced equipment and are confident in your skills, have your own hand at it. Just remember this is one of those scenarios when bringing in the professionals pays off.

Shape a Virtual Tour.
The time your customers spend is precious and they want to learn as much about a property as possible before they visit in person. Virtual tours are a great way to give potential buyers a comprehensive, accurate forecast of the property.

Central Patronage.
Consider sponsoring local festivals, sporting teams or school events. Signing up as a local

sponsor often means getting a spot-on t-shirt, program brochures or flyers for your business. Want additional tips?

Animated video.
Consider outsourcing your real estate business to a quality animated video. Quick, adorable, high-quality cartoon videos will help set up your brand and add a touch of personality to it. You may also want to find your animated video featuring local landmarks or locations to make it ultra-unique and targeted.
You don't have to be super complex with your animated video – check out this short and very basic animated Geico commercial.

Pinterest Galleries.
Pinterest boards are a great way to provide the specific listings with images and information. For a single property, you can create a Pinterest board that, in addition to photos of the property, highlights the area's major benefits.

Make Mobile-Friendly Your Blog.
Tech-savvy customers are investing lots of time on their computers. Indeed, a recent study showed that 80 % of Internet users are using their mobile devices for online activity. Your website is mobile friendly, it's important. Even better, consider creating a mobile app which could be used by potential buyers to review listings.

Make a Newsletter.

Email marketing is one of the best strategies for establishing relationships with clients. Collect emails from your website, local browsing, or any other methods you might think about. Send your email subscribers the stuff they 're looking for – announcements of upcoming open houses, new houses on the market, news of seminars you 're offering in the region, etc. (Note: if you're working in various geographic areas, you'll want to segment your newsletter subscribers based on their location, making sure they 're getting only specific emails and updates from you.)

Build My Business Page on Google.
Google My Business is Google's latest on location-based pages. Do not worry if you feel confused – it's basically the same idea as Google Places for Business and Google+ Pages. Setting up a Google My Business account makes Google Search, Google Maps and Google+ easy for users to find you. This one is a no-brainer, believe me.
Google my guide to business

Think of Going Niche.
If you have some competition in your area for real estate marketing, you might want to consider making yourself stand out by going niche. Make yourself the go-to real estate agent for dog owners, families with children, divorced people, whatever. Making a name for yourself regarding a particular need for a niche can make you memorable, especially in saturated zip codes.

Use Storytelling Emotional.

Use emotional storytelling with powerful visual elements and compelling copy. People respond to stories-tell a good one and customers flock to you.

Hosting a Webinar.

Hosting a webinar can be a perfect way to attract publicity for your company if you feel confident enough. Host a webinar entitled "12 Little-Known Things To Look For In A New Home," which will provide a Q&A for questions at the end. Webinars can also be repurposed as YouTube videos, and can serve as useful video material that can live on your website permanently! Here are some more tips on making a perfect webinar put together.

Saddle up for advertising on social issues.

Don't be afraid of dishing dough on social media for paid ads. Despite organic influence dwindling on many popular social networks such as Facebook, paid Facebook ads are also the most productive way of getting in front of customers. Facebook has tons of great targeting features that make sure you 're only paying to get your target audiences noticed.

Old Mailers in School.

The web is where it is, but that is not to say that traditional advertising has no place, especially if you have target audiences. Try sending out postcards in the different zip codes you 're interested in to eligible leads or potential buyers.

Become a Local Magazine Columnist.
As far as real estate is concerned, it is important that you focus on the local laser. Running ads in local newspapers or magazines is a perfect way to get the word out about you and your company. See if the local publications can write a column or feature. You don't want to be overtly salesy-buyers today don't like being sold to. Seek to highlight your expertise instead. Write about how rising housing prices on the market show the city is doing well, or list the reasons why your regional area is becoming more popular (maybe it's the revitalized downtown area or better school system).

Host Free Home Buyer Seminar.
Hosting mini-seminars makes yourself and your knowledge available to the community. Consider delivering a clear 101 seminar on the basics of home ownership and mortgages.
Know, it's all about inbound marketing today and it doesn't just happen online. Before you invest time and money in you, users want you to share some of your knowledge for free. A seminar on home buying is the local equivalent of a webinar. Sure, it will take time and effort, but impressed attendees are going to walk away and have formed a friendship with you. That relationship, when they are ready to shop for a home, will be worth its weight in gold.

Get the mark.
Branding is your friend-meaning pens, drink koozies, and enjoy all those other freebies. Offer

some branded goodies to spread your brand at local festivals and events.
Real estate marketing consultancy

Partner with Local Businesses.
The development of relationships with other local businesses will be key to your marketing efforts in real estate. See if you can purchase local breakfast joints to allow you to purchase a set of new coffee mugs with your logo on them, or buy a place on their place mate setting. Don't worry about getting creative with local partnerships.

Ask for Testimonials from Former Clients.
Testimonials are tremendous trust signals. Showing real, live people endorsing your services means the world for potential customers. When a homebuyer has had a great experience with you, reach out to them and ask for a testimonial. If possible, try to get a photo of them as well. Make the most of these testimonials by placing them strategically on your website and sharing them now and then on social networks.

Building an impressive website.
Consumers of today tend to do a lot of legwork themselves online while making major transactions, and this also involves purchasing house. I've only rented myself, but even when renting a property I 'm going to google map the address, use Street View to get a feel for the city, see which businesses are within walking distance, take a look at home pictures and, hopefully, take a virtual property tour. Make access to all this

information easy for users – make sure all your property pages have great photos, virtual tours and easy access to Google Maps and Google Earth. List the nearby hot spots and their respective walking distances (mention the bus stop which is only a five-minute walk away, or the Starbucks at the end of the block).

Make it easy to navigate your Site.
All of the world's great property sites won't mean much if your site is a nightmare to browse. Your visitors need to have a good website experience so take the time to brush up on the design skills and information architecture of the user experience.

Have Copy Local-Oriented.
Make sure you include some local-oriented keywords in your copy to ensure that the buyers Googling online find your content for homes in your area.

Getting on Zillow.
Zillow is basically the Yelp of real estate marketing and if you want some chance to be discovered you really need to be there-you can disregard the heat, but it will always burn you! Zillow gives the website the right to advertise as an agent. It can get a little pricey, but given the tremendous position Zillow plays in buying a home, it is probably your best bet. Sites like Zillow account for 48 percent of all real estate search site traffic on the internet, after all. Also, Zillow allows users to review real estate agents, so put that rating on

a smile and rack up as a solid star rating will greatly increase your lead.

Shared Device Scheduling.
To show buyers a house using a scheduling sharing app to coordinate times. Scheduling applications such as Doodle can reduce slot swapping on endless back and forth time.

Give a Package for Local Care after closing.
Your commitment to a customer doesn't end immediately after they close. You want them to remember your name so that they will hopefully share your information with friends, family and acquaintances who might be considering moving forward. After they close, send customers a local care package with local movie or theater tickets, restaurant gift cards, etc.

Hold tactful.
Stay in touch with past buyers (even months and years later), to build on that good relationship. To stay fresh in their minds, send anniversary cards, holiday cards etc. If they have a friend ready to buy, they'll pass your details along. Provide opportunities to refer you to prospective homebuyers for past clients.
Taking advantage of Call Tracking.
Real estate is one of those industries that their paid search campaigns absolutely must use call tracking. When trying to find a realtor or make an appointment, most people use the phone to view an apartment, condo or house. If those calls happen because someone has seen your PPC

ad, then you want to be able to monitor which advertisements and

INTERNET AND WEBSITE
Internet Marketing for Real Estate Agents

It's becoming more and more than just a website, an successful Facebook business page and a mediocre real estate blog (you can't just rely on the real estate site of your company). You need laser sharp strategies to find fresh leads and great sales chances. Now is the time to market yourself online and reap the advantages of internet real estate marketing. Let us see some procedural steps that can be followed to achieve this;

Web Design Responsive (Mobile Friendly)
When more people access content online with mobile devices such as smartphones, you have to make sure the web pages stand out on the smaller screen. It would also be fair to say that more than 50 percent of your web visitors to your real estate web come from a mobile device or laptop right now. Prospective houses are fundamentally visual and have to be seen to draw prospects in their best light. Your own architecture must therefore be flexible, i.e. your images and text must be transferred seamlessly

from conventional desktops to smaller devices. Since customers will enjoy the usability of your website from different platforms, responsive user design can turn into more views, leads and sales. Attractive cover art, for example, can add sizzle to both your social media profile and your mobile pages. You'll also want to make sure that you customize your email for mobile marketing and stick to best practices in mobile email marketing. What does a mobile computer look like on your website? If it's not good, hard to read, and not optimized, you 're losing leads, listings, and sales for sure.

Sticking to the local market
Using the power of online real estate platforms these days will help you reach for different

markets. Both buyers (especially tech-savvy, first-time buyers) and sellers like to spend as many hours researching prospective homes at their leisure as they need. Meet them where they're most spending time. People in a local market want real estate agents to produce details about demographics and characteristics of the neighborhood including:

- Schools and kindergartens
- Fiscal rates and estimates
- Housing ranges
- Types of Properties

The more relevant information you can generally provide the better.

Build the Prospect and Buyers email list

You may not convert a visitor into a house buyer overnight, but if you capture their contact information, you will have the chance to make an impression over several weeks or months (or even years) as a real estate expert. E-mail real estate marketing can be an effective tool for open house invitations, monthly market updates and providing useful tips for transitional people. People may not be willing to buy or sell right now, but when they are you will have top-of-the-mind experience and be their go-to agent because you have kept in constant touch with useful information and identified yourself as the authority in your business. Not only that, it can also lead to more referrals from the people you keep up-to - date with your real estate email newsletter.

Encourage consumer feedback on real estate pages with heavy traffic

Once you complete housing transactions successfully, it's important to use the positive relationships you've built to create your credibility. In addition to keeping a profile on the best networks for home listing, invite your clients to request a sample of their work. Each month websites such as Zillow.com and Homes.com get millions of views, and all of this traffic is aimed at home professionals like you. Turn best reviews on your website into testimonials. This will help you get higher search engine rankings as well as make you stand out as the go-to person in your local market by declaring your company on Google and getting feedback there.

Using growing, attractive picture covers

Houses are meant to be showcased from both indoors and outdoors, so use your real estate funnel front-end to show them in their best light. It's useful to add a link because people can access specific details about your listed homes, or a mobile app, or an upcoming event.

Answer Real Estate discussion forums and Local Facebook Community questions

Forums for buyers, sellers and real estate agents remain common and successful meeting points. Answering a few well-answered questions will improve your credibility and inspire people to visit your social media profiles elsewhere. They may even wish to meet you personally, eventually. Discipline yourself to (at most) use thirty (30) minutes per day to answer good questions and engage with potential customers. Another great opportunity is to join the community's local Facebook groups, and also be a valuable tool. You'd be shocked how many leads you can produce from social media free of buyers and sellers.

Optimize the speed of your website
Make sure your website is speed-optimized. Especially when it comes to real estate, which will include multiple high-quality images that take longer to load, it's important to make sure your website loads quickly. A faster website will increase the likelihood of people staying on your website and will also help your website to rank higher in search engines, which will result in more visitors, leads, listings and ultimately sales

"Your Website is your best tool for marketing"

- Use SEO to Improve Your Organic Rank in Search Engines
- Engage Your Visitors with Visuals
- Use Clear Navigation
- Update Your Content
- Offer Value to Your Visitors
- Put a Blog on Your Site & Post Consistently
- Keep Branding Consistent
- Integrate Your Social Media & Email Marketing Strategy
- Make it Mobile-Friendly.

SIGNAGE

Signage systems are information systems that are visually oriented, consisting of signs, maps, arrows, color coding systems, pictograms and various typographic elements; Signage systems vary from other information delivery approaches as they are usually used to direct people's passage across the physical world; road signs on a highway, subway station identification signs and overhead signs at an airport are all common examples of signage systems. Wayfinding, way signing or signposting is known as the act of following a signage system.

Signage is often a leading marketing source of inquiry in real estate development. It is always debatable whether it is the primary source of enquiry or acts as a complement to another source. Signage is thus an important marketing tool for residential, industrial and retirement projects. Signage is also the topic of debate within project meetings. Marketers sometimes hear the war cry of 'just get the signs up' or 'we need more signage,' but there's a lot to consider and it's something it needs a strategic and concerted effort at the top.

- Location, location, location.
- Structural considerations.
- Signage permits.
- Messaging - Keep it simple!
- Imagery – Stand out from the rest.
- Directional and way finding signage
- Destination signage

- Flags and banners.
- Landscaping and maintenance
- Timing

Watch out for all these when setting up a website for your brand.

CHAPTER 5
TENANT DATA MANAGEMENT

The term "multitenancy software" refers to a software architecture in which one instance of software operates on a computer, serving multiple tenants. These engineered systems are also called shared (unlike dedicated or isolated) systems. A tenant is a group of users who share a common access to the software instance with particular privileges. A software application is designed with a multitenant architecture to provide each tenant with a dedicated share of the instance-including its data, configuration, user management, individual tenant functionality and non-functional properties. Multitenancy compares with multi-instance systems, where different instances of software function on behalf of various tenants

When a multi-tenancy Data Management system is set up, users can associate their profiles with more than one company. Users can create jobs and templates for these businesses, and can use the custom templates created for the businesses. Custom templates can be added to multiple companies so they can share the templates.

Developing a database structure that can accommodate this type of design depends on several factors including:

- Client data isolation
- Database scalability
- Security
- Database management (backup and restoration)
- Operational complexities such as schema and tenant management
- Speed.

Depending on your requirements, there are a few different ways to design your database I will explain those below.

- Database-per-tenant
- Multi-tenant database
- Single multi-tenant database
- Shared multi-tenant database

Database-per-tenant

A tenant (organization) has its own database, as the name implies. Each time a new tenant is added to the system, the user generates a new database. Each time a new tenant is added, a new schema is generated which creates a separate tenant database.

This structure facilitates tenant-level customization and proper isolation of the data. This design's query speed is relatively ok, as the search path to the tenant database is set before queries are executed. The benefits of this design include simple data backup, reconstruction, and migration.

This architecture provides isolation and speed of the data, but it does not scale so well. This design is successful when the number of tenants / clients on the system is low but when tenants are larger, resource compromises are bound to occur. The number of tables increases, the number of queries increases, the size of those tables also increases. As more tenants are added, therefore, there is a need for continued resource scaling.

Multi-tenant database

This design allows many tenants (of any number) access to a multi-tenant database. Because data isolation is not met by storing several tenants in a multi-tenant database, the database scheme contains a column of tenant identification that is used in the database to identify each tenant. That is the method used to isolate data relating to tenants and to retrieve data.

With this design system resources are better managed because the shares of the multi-tenant database compute resources and store resources across all tenants. A disadvantage of sharing resources between different tenants is that there is no way to monitor each tenant's use of these resources and workload and this can cause the server to be crippled.

Single multi-tenant database

The architecture makes it easier for all tenants to use a single database. Calculation and storage resources are increased as more tenants are added.

The big downside of this design is that the database is easily manageable and complex. Management activities are incredibly difficult for each tenant to conduct. Also, if all tenants access the database and run queries in the same database, it could affect the speed of query operation.

Shared multi-tenant database

This architecture allows the distribution of tenant data through several repositories (shards), with all of the data stored in a single shard for a specific tenant. The database schema handles and applies a sharing key / tenant identifier.

This design provides high scalability, and the databases can also be easily managed by distributing tenants across several small databases. It also operates cost-effectively

Given the need to maintain a mapping between tenants and databases, designing the shard architecture may be complex. The application also needs to hold a list of the shards and their respective tenants. Besides the multi-tenancy nature of the database, the data base structure is often included in multi-tenancy applications.

Catalog-based multitenancy -- In order to facilitate data isolation, a tenant has its own database catalog with the tenant identifier. This could be expensive to operate and maintain.

Schema-based multitenancy -- In order to facilitate data isolation, a tenant has its own database scheme with the tenant identifier. This can be costly in terms of computing if the database sits on a single physical server and Neighbor noise can be an obstacle.

Table-based multitenancy — Multiple tenants are clustered in the same database with tenant identification specified on a column of identifiers that is added to all tables to facilitate data isolation. Like any other single tenancy database, the database can be handled but the application traffic to the database is heavy, and management operations are difficult.

Virtualization and scaling for multi-tenant application

Once you've designed your database, and you should be able to put some thought into Scaling. I'm not saying build some complex network structures before you have proof of concept, but it's good to have an understanding and plan in place to increase the multi-tenant application's computing resources to meet the increase in application demand and traffic, as more tenants are added. Scaling can be achieved through either a vertical or horizontal scaling.

Vertical scalability — In a system, it involves increasing resources on a single node. The resources might be additional CPUs, memory, or other components that could increase system speed. It is considered the first step toward scaling. To benefit fully from vertical scaling, it is necessary that the multi-tenant app's architecture is well designed to make optimal use of available resources and maintain asynchronicity among all application components.

Horizontal scalability — This is taken into account when deploying the application in a distributed architecture with multiple instances of the service running on many nodes. By adding more machines to the pool of resources, horizontal scaling simply increases the number of instances and nodes. Increasing the number of instances leads to future load balancing needs. Horizontal scaling is not restricted, and fault toleration and data isolation are facilitated. A few techniques were introduced to handle the implementation of multi-tenant applications. Physical separation can be used to give each tenant their own dedicated hardware resources, or virtualization to create virtual hosting environments for each client but on the same physical resources, or to design the application to automatically adapt to different tenants at runtime.

Virtualization involves the use of software to create application hosting environments which provide logical boundaries between each tenant with tenants sharing virtual separation computing resources. That can be achieved through:

Virtual machine technology — it provides an emulator for running multiple operating systems on a hardware while sharing the same physical hardware on it.

Virtualization of user session — allocates computing resources dynamically to user session within a multi-user operating system.

Application pools — they're sandboxes on the server side to isolate application processes. Each pool consists of a collection of processes for the operating systems.

Client-side application sand boxing — applications can be loaded into a client-side execution sandbox and run within a virtual runtime environment of the application.

TENANTS MOVE-IN

Let us analyze some legal procedural steps to take while a tenant Is moving in or moving out, and how this relates to a landlord;

Rights and Duties of Landlords

The legislation imposes a number of obligations on the landlord and confers a number of reciprocal privileges on the tenant. These include

(1) possession,
(2) habitable status,
(3) non-interference with use.

(1) possession,
The landlord must grant the landowner the right to own the property. This duty is infringed if, at the time the tenant is entitled to take possession of the property, a third party has overriding title to the property and the declaration of this title will deprive the tenant of the use envisaged by the parties. Paramount title means any legitimate

interest in the premises that is not terminable at the landlord's will or at the time the tenant is entitled to take possession of the property. If the occupant has already taken possession of the property and only learns the paramount title, or if the paramount title comes into being only only, the landlord will not actually be in violation. If the occupant is subsequently evicted from the premises and thereby stripped of the house, however, then the landlord is in violation. Suppose the landlord has rented a house to a doctor for ten years, knowing the doctor intends to open a medical office in part of the house and also knowing that the lot is restricted to residential uses only. Physician comes in. The landlord is not on default yet. If a neighbor obtains an injunction against keeping the property, the landlord would be in default. But if the landlord did not know (and should not possibly have known) that the doctor wanted to use his home for an office, then the landlord would not be in default under the contract, because the property could have been put to regular – that is, residential – use without jeopardizing the tenant's right of ownership.

(2) habitable status,
As applied to rentals, the old caveat emptor common-law doctrine said she will take the premises as she considers them until the occupant has signed the lease. She shouldn't complain later, as she could inspect them before signing the lease. In addition, if hidden defects come to light, they should be easy enough to fix

the tenant herself. This law no longer applies to residential rentals, at least, today. Unless the parties expressly agree otherwise, if the conditions are unsuitable for residential use when the tenant is due to move in, the landlord will be in breach of his lease. The landlord is kept on an implicit habitability pledge. The change in the rule is due in part to the conditions of the modern urban setting: in areas where housing is scarce, tenants have little or no power to walk away from an available apartment. It is also due to the construction of modems and the technology: few tenants can fix most types of defects. The following has been said by a US appeals court. Today's urban tenants, the vast majority of whom live in multiple dwelling houses, are not interested in the land, but only in "a house suitable for occupation." Moreover, today's urban dweller usually has a single, specialized skill unrelated to maintenance work; he is unable to make reparations such as the "jack-of-all-trades" farmer who was the lessee's common law model. Furthermore, unlike his agrarian predecessor who mostly resided for his entire life on one piece of land, today urban tenants are more mobile than ever before. Sometimes, tenure of a resident in a specific apartment would not be enough to justify attempts at repairs. Moreover, the increasing complexity of the dwellings today makes them much harder to repair than the structures of the earlier times. In a multiple dwelling, repairs may require landlord-controlled access to equipment and areas.

(3) non-interference with use.

In addition to the physically appropriate maintenance of the premises, the landlord has an obligation to the tenant not to interfere with the permissible use of the premises. Suppose Simone moves into multi-apartment house. One of the other tenants plays music consistently late into the evening, causing Simone to lose sleep. She complains to the landlord, who has a lease provision which allows him to terminate any tenant who persists in disturbing other tenants. If the landlord doesn't do anything after Simone notifies him of the disturbance, he'll be in violation. It is often claimed that this right to be free of interference with acceptable uses derives from the implicit promise of peaceful enjoyment by the landlord.

Issues to Address Before New Tenant Move In
Repair any damage or safety and health issues
A landlord is obliged to keep the property for rental. You'll want to repair any existing damage, health or safety problems at the property before a tenant moves in.

Clean Property
Cleaning is particularly important if you're doing an apartment turnover, which means a previous tenant has been living in the unit. You 're going to want to make sure that the unit is thoroughly cleaned, especially areas such as the tub, toilet, stove and fridge. Vacuum or sweep away any further debris.

Look for Heating, Plumbing or Electric Problems
You must ensure all utilities are working before a tenant moves in. You will want to ensure that the heat works in all the rooms, that there are no clogs or leaks in the plumbing and that the outlets and overhead lights are operational in every room. These are needing a tenant needs to sustain its quality of life.

Check and register lease with landlord
You should go over the section by section of the lease agreement with the tenant so they fully understand what they agree to. Once you have been through the entire arrangement with the tenant and answered any questions, you and the tenant should sign the lease agreement and date it.

Collect Rent and Security Deposits for the first month
You should always collect the rent for the first month and all of the security deposit before the tenant moves into the unit. If the tenant receives government assistance, such as Section 8, the exception to collecting the first month's rent prior to moving in would be Section 8 sends the check to you after the tenant has moved into the unit.

Had land inspections done
Depending on the laws of your town, a home inspector might need to inspect the unit before a tenant can move in. This inspection is done so that the town can give you a Habitability Certificate. Some towns require this inspection

only when the unit is rented for the first time, some towns require it every five years and some require it each time a new tenant moves into the unit. Make sure you know the rules that apply to your town.

Switch Locks
You should always change the locks at the doors before a new tenant is moving in. This is done for the tenant's protection, and to protect you against liability. You don't want to have the keys to the new tenant 's apartment from an old tenant. Spend the $20 on a new lock to prevent any issues.

Go through the checklist for moves in
On the actual move-in day of the tenant, you should go over the checklist of the move-in which describes in detail the condition of the property as a whole and of each room. You should have the checklist with the tenant sign and date. The moving-in checklist is relevant because it helps you to compare the property's condition when the tenant moves in, with the property 's condition when the tenant moves out.

RENT AND SECURITY DEPOSITS
A security deposit is money that is given as evidence of intent to move in and care for the home to a landlord, lender, or seller of a home or apartment. Deposits for insurance can be either refundable or non-refundable, depending on the terms of the agreement. A security deposit is

intended for the receiver as a guarantee of protection, and may also be used to pay for losses or missing property. Security deposits serve as an intangible measure of security in the event of damages or lost property, or as a means of tangible security.

"States have varying laws on where a security deposit is held, such as separate banking or escrow account and whether it"

Security deposits are paid prior to moving into or taking possession of the property and typically these deposits are the same amount as the monthly rent. A security deposit may be used to repair or remove equipment in a rental unit if the losses originated from the renter 's actions.

For example, if a renter breaks a window or does permanent harm to the property's floors , walls or facilities, then the landlord can use the security deposit for repair purposes. Usually, when the property is in good shape, and when the renter moves out, the security deposit will be refunded to them without the need for maintenance.

A security deposit serves as a means of fixing or replacing something that had been damaged, lost or stolen by the renter in a rental unit. Typically, security deposits are refunded upon departure if the property remains in 'reasonably' good shape—to the point of normal depreciation). Typically, security deposits must be paid before moving in and state laws dictate how security deposits are applied when necessary.

Basics of safe deposits at rental property
A security deposit is a one-time, refundable amount of money that a landlord receives from a tenant in addition to the rent they make for their first month. Collecting a security deposit is not required by law but it can help protect you financially if a tenant causes rental damage or leaves without paying rent unexpectedly. While your state may restrict how much you can collect, all states allow you to collect an amount equal to the rent for at least one month. Let us take a close look into this.

State Deposit Limits
Both U.S. states require landlords to obtain security deposits, and the maximum sum depends on where the property is located.

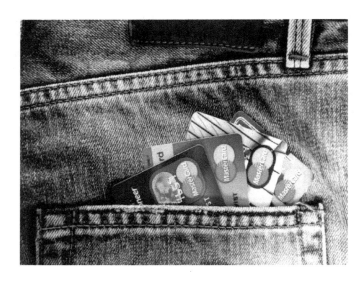

Some states have no limit to how much can be

obtained, such as Illinois and Texas. In Connecticut, as a security deposit, landlords can't require more than two months' rent. When a resident is 62 years of age or older, this cap is limited to one month's rent.1 Other states allow landlords to charge tenants up to anywhere from one to three months' rent.

Deposits Date of arrival
Before a tenant moves into a rental, collect the entire security deposit. This should be a lease condition, so if a tenant is unable to provide the full amount in advance, you can cancel the lease and rent to another prospective tenant who has also been screened thoroughly.

Deposits Stocks
Many states do not control where security deposits must be deposited, but others mandate that you put each deposit in a separate interest-bearing account.

Security deposits aren't landlord income. They are funds that both parties agree to set aside, through a lease, for expenses that tenants may or may not incur at a future date.
Some states also require that you give a tenant a receipt of the security deposit within 30 days of moving-in. The receipt must identify the bank and the annual interest rate where the deposit is held. Many states go a step further and mandate that you disclose the interest accrued on the security deposit annually.

Deposits refunded
-- state has a different law about how long landlords are expected to either refund security deposits or specify reasons for keeping them. Some set the limit at 15 days after the lease is over, while others give you up to 30 days to return the deposit or send a written notice to the owner as to why it has not been returned.

Keeping Drops
A security deposit is a kind of landlord protection, because it covers the tenant against a breach of the contract. Although you are allowed to sue a tenant for the money that they owe you, it is often difficult to collect the money even if you are given the judgment against them. Security deposits offer a buffer for softening the blow of lost revenue.

TENANT ON SCREENING

Tenant screening is a process that residential landlords and property managers use mainly to assess prospective tenants. The aim is to determine the probability that the occupant will follow the terms of the lease or rental agreement and will also take great care of the property concerned. The process culminates in a decision about whether to sanction the applicant, conditionally accept the applicant (such as having an increased deposit or co-signer) or refuse tenancy.

Usually, the tenant screening process starts when the prospective tenant (each adult applicant) completes a rental application, pays a fee for the application and maybe a holding deposit.

The purpose of rental applications is to collect personal identifying information (name, social security number and date of birth, etc.), address, employment, criminal history and eviction. A signature is generally required, which certifies the accuracy of the information provided, agrees to certain terms and conditions and authorizes the procurement of a screening report for tenants.

Screening of tenants is an integral part of a risk-based property management approach. Read on to discover why establishing a structured screening procedure and consistently implementing it would help your property management company to uphold the highest standards and stay consistent with all fair housing laws.

Tenant screening is the process of looking at the context and past of someone before making a real estate transaction, like signing a contract. A rigorous screening process identifies potential "red flags" and offers opportunities to enhance your customer service-both critical to building beneficial long-term relationships with current and prospective tenants. The screening process can be informal, such as a question checklist for prospective tenants to ask, or a more detailed report collection and information review to help you make the decision. The important thing is to ensure that you have a clear, well-thought-out policy which is consistently used with each new applicant and applied in the same way.

TENANT SCREENING REPORT

Screening reports for tenants include one or more of the following elements:

Report on consumer credit (with or without a score)-from one of the three national credit bureaus (Experian , Equifax or Transunion).
Disposal records search
Check criminal history
Search for sex offender registry
Specially designated searches of nationals (often referred to as OFAC searches)
Rental accommodations
Employment Checks
Recommendation-based on criteria(parameters) of the landlord;

Credit reports and searches for databases are often sent back instantly via secure websites. Additional information resulting from more thorough searches of public records, rental references and job verifications can take somewhere from a few hours to a few days.

REVIEW OF RENTS

Rent reviews allow for the periodic adjustment of commercial rents to the current market level as of the review date.

They are held at whatever intervals agreed in the commercial lease rent approval clause(s).

Rent reviews typically take place every three to five years, a frequency that has reflected the recent general shortening of lease lengths.
Commercial leases historically were issued in the UK for 20 years or more. Rent approval provisions were implemented after World War II to counter high rates of inflation, and were at intervals of seven to 14 years up to the 1960s. Shorter 10 to 15-year leases are now more popular with landlords and tenants.

The rent review clause sets out when each review will take place, the review method, the assumptions and disregards to be made when valuing the premises for rent review purposes, the procedure to be followed and the dispute resolution provisions if they arise.

Open-market revaluation is the most common method of recalculating a trade rent at the review date.
When parties are unable to compromise on a new contract, the lease negotiation clause typically stipulates a process for a — for instance the.
Bad rent reviews will result in financial loss, stalemate in negotiating new rents and even termination of the contract.

Chartered valuation surveyors specializing in commercial rent reviews can successfully act in commercial rent review matters on behalf of landlords or tenants.

TYPES OF RENT REVIEWS
Let us look into the Types of rent reviews we have.

A standard commercial lease will provide for a review of open market rents. A different rent review method will be specified, though, sometimes. Alternatives include fixed increases, an index-linked review or a rent-link to the tenant 's business turnover.

Open-market review

An open market review means adjusting the rent (usually only upwards) to reflect the rent that the landlord could accomplish on a letting in the open market.

The provisions of the rent review will specify the terms of a "hypothetical lease" that must be valued to arrive at the new rental figure. It is necessary to specify the length of the hypothetical lease term, because the rental value may vary depending on whether a 5 year or 10-year term is on offer. In order to ensure fairness there will also be different "assumptions" and "disregards."

Hypotheses generally include the tenant 's compliance with his covenants (so that the tenant does not benefit from a rent reduction because he has failed to keep the premises in repair) and that, if the premises were damaged by an insured risk, they were reinstated.

Hikes in fixed leases

Increases in fixed rentals are uncommon but can be seen in short leases or leases on unique premises or premises that are difficult to value. In the lease is stated the rent for each year or number of years, e.g. £10,000 for year 1, £12,000 for years 2-4 and £15,000 for years 5-7.

Rent analysis related to index

With index-linked reviews, by reference to an index such as the Retail Prices Index or Consumer Prices Index, the rent is increased (or sometimes decreased) Such reviews are not common but can be found in short leases or leases of premises that are not easy to value, as with fixed rent increases.

Leases on turnover

Rent is occasionally linked to the tenant's turnover. The rent might be entirely linked to turnover, or a mixture of a percentage of market rent and a "uplift" of turnover rent might be present.
The landlord requires complete and timely disclosure of the tenant's trading accounts to get a turnover rent assessment to operate. A turnover rent review is more difficult and time-consuming to conduct than other forms of rent review but in

certain situations the sense of relationship it creates between landlord and tenant would be appealing to the parties.

CHAPTER 6
PROPERTY AND FINANCE
REPORTS

A Financial Statement is a sworn or affirmed document in the form of an affidavit, and the party swearing or affirming the Financial Statement must be satisfied that the Statement's contents are true and correct, and that the party has no other income, assets or financial resources not included in the Financial Statement. Any omissions made by the Financial Statement, such as failing to include a property held in its name or having an interest in it, may have serious consequences for that party, such as concerns

about creditworthiness at a final hearing. Where the financial status of a party shifts throughout the litigation, the party must file an amended financial statement setting out the current financial circumstances. An accurate Financial Statement is imperative. We encourage you to make an appointment to talk about your financial statement with one of our Family Law Solicitors.

We know that unnecessary costs need to be cut from operations when managing the income generating real estate assets. We know that expenditure should be reduced wherever possible. We know that to raise sales we will take full advantage of new income sources and rising rentals and fees. When performing these tasks correctly, a property 's income potential will be maximized.

As an owner of investment property, you must know more about the financial state of your land. It is important to hire the right property asset manager to preserve and increase the value of your properties, and to provide reliable, comprehensive financial reports so that you can monitor your financial goals. Financial reporting includes all the financial information that a company communicates to people outside the company.

Here are six financial reports which your property manager should provide each month:

- Balance sheet: This is a snapshot of a property's financial status as of report date. It is a summary of the owner's assets, liabilities, and equities. At a glance, you will see real balances in bank accounts, cumulative sums of delinquency and vacancy, equity deposits retained, the sum owed to others, transfers of ownership made and much more.

- Monthly income and expenditure statement: This report should have a detailed month-to-date and year-to-date income breakdown and itemized expenditure with a comparison of the budgeted numbers. A budget is your guideline for the operation of your asset when properly generated and used. You will be able to expect the property to deliver on that budget. Being able to compare actual budget figures lets you know if you are achieving the budgeted objectives.

- General ledger: This provides a detailed record of individual transactions resulting in total numbers reflected in the balance sheet and statement of revenues and expenses. Every entry has to be self-explanatory. If you see numerous corrections in different accounts every month, or frequent entries to a clearing account with vague descriptions, ask your manager.

- Accounts payable report: This should include all payments for debts and other financial obligations made during the reporting period.

The aim is to provide a clear audit trail for each property for all funds. Look for a business that keeps copies of all invoices, and is happy to support you.

- Tenant receivables and prepaid report(s): This document lists the overdue and prepaid accounts of individual tenants outlined in the balance sheet and statement of income / expense.
- Copy of monthly bank statements with reconciliations: This will substantiate the balance of bank accounts reflected in the balance sheet as well as the deposits and debits reflected in the general ledger.

Briefly discussing various financial statements to make understanding this subject more concrete,

Income statement

The income statement, which shows net income or net loss, is one of four types of financial reports. This type of statement tracks all the money that comes in, and all the money that goes out. Money paid out is called expenses and the money that comes in is called income. When the expenses exceed the revenue, a net loss will be shown on the income statement. The statement of income shall be divided into categories including:

- Advertising
- Operating Costs

- Non-operating costs

Operating expenses include advertising, and office space rentals. Non-operating costs may include a one-time payment of borrowed money and interest. Sales include the cost of all merchandise sold.

Balance sheet

The balance sheet is another of the four types of financial statements and this one seems to be the most ignored of all the types of financial statements out there. Entrepreneurs are intrigued by the income statement but turn a disinterested eye to other financial reporting elements such as the balance sheet. It is also unfortunate as this is one of the most important kinds of financial reports.

The balance sheet contains the capital assets, liabilities, and equity of owners or shareholders. The assets include cash, real estate, inventory, and anything else the company owns. Assets are listed on the balance sheet left hand side. Liabilities and equity are shown on the right-hand side. Liabilities include accounts payable, or some sort of long-term loan payment.

Equity of the owners or shareholders is determined when the amount of liabilities is subtracted from the sum of the properties. The reason the formula is called a balance sheet is because it will always look like this:

Assets = Assets + Shareholders' Equities

Cash-flow analysis

The third of the four big financial statements is the cash flow statement. This financial statement on the company aims to accomplish one thing: tell you where all your cash went. The financial reporting components can get a little complicated on this one, so if you don't have four years of accounting education it may be hard to understand. The number of categories on this statement can vary depending on the size of the company. The categories for bigger companies include:

- Working activities
- Activities investing
- Financing operations
- Additional information

There are only two groups for smaller companies: cash inflows, and capital outflows. The fundamental idea of the cash flow statement is to know and understand exactly where cash flows from and where it flows to. It allows the firm to see if they spend more than they earn, or vice versa. If the revenue sum is significantly higher than the net profit, this means that the net profit of the organization is "good quality."

Owner's equity declaration

If there are any changes in owner's equity between accounting periods, they will be listed on the owner's equity statement, the fourth of the major financial statements. The key components listed herein include:

- Balance beginning with equity
- Additions and suspensions
- End of equilibrium

Additions and subtractions are for a specific period of time and may include things such as net income, dividend payments, and withdrawals.

ASSET LIST REPORT

An asset is an economic-value resource owned or controlled by an individual, corporation, or country with the expectation that it will deliver a future benefit. Assets are listed on the balance sheet of a company and are acquired or produced to increase the value of a company or support the operations of that company. An asset can be thought of as something that, in the future, can generate cash flow, reduce expenses, or improve sales, regardless of whether it's manufacturing equipment or a patent.

An asset is an economic-value resource owned or controlled by an individual, corporation, or country with the expectation that it will deliver a future benefit. Assets are listed on the balance sheet of a company and are acquired or produced to increase the value of a company or support the operations of that company. An asset can be seen as something that can generate cash flow in the future, reduce expenses or improve sales, irrespective of whether it's manufacturing equipment or a patent.

An asset also an economic resource that an person, company, or country may possess. Assets are expected to offer potential economic benefits, such as:

- Value rise for an organization or nation
- Net added value for one person

Assets achieve so by generating cash flow, reducing costs and/or rising revenue.

An asset represents an economic advantage for a business or represents exposure that other individuals or companies do not have. A right or other access is legally enforceable, ensuring that an individual may use economic resources at the discretion of a corporation and its use may be precluded or restricted.

In order for an asset to be available, a firm must have a right to it from the date of the financial statements. An economic resource is something that is scarce and has the potential to generate economic gain by producing cash inflows or through cash outflows.

Assets can be broadly categorized into short-term (or current) assets, fixed assets, financial investments, and intangible assets.

Types of assets

Current Assets

Current assets are short-term economic capital which can be turned into cash in one year. Current assets include cash and cash equivalents, receivable accounts, inventories and various prepayment expenses.

While cash is easy to appraisal, accountants periodically reassess inventory recoverability and receivable accounts. If there is evidence that the receivable accounts could be uncollectible, it will become impaired. Or if the inventory becomes obsolete, those assets may be written off by companies. Assets are reported in the balance sheets of companies based on the historical cost model, which measures the asset's original cost, adjusted for any changes or aging.

Fixed Property

Fixed assets, such as plants, equipment, and buildings, are long-term resources. An adjustment for the aging of fixed assets is made on the basis of periodic charges called depreciation, which may or may not reflect the loss of a fixed asset's earning power. Under two broad approaches, the commonly accepted accounting principles

(GAAP) allow for depreciation. The straight-line method assumes that a fixed asset loses its value in proportion to its useful life, while the accelerated method assumes that in its first years of use, the asset loses its value more rapidly.

Financial assets

Financial assets account for investments in other institutions' properties and securities. Financial assets comprise stocks, corporate and sovereign bonds, preferred equity and other hybrid securities. Financial assets are measured according to the categorization of the investment and the reason behind it.

Intangible Properties

Intangible assets are economic resources where physical presence is not present. Patents, trademarks, copyrights and goodwill are included. Intangible asset accounting varies depending on the type of asset, and they may either be amortized or checked for loss each year.

BLANK REPORTS

The Blank Report lets you build your own report from scratch. It includes the same layout editor as our other new reports, so you can add calendars and groups of accounts, formulas, rules for switching, and columns for date and comparison. You can also include blocks of text and notes in your report.

EXPENSES REPORT

Specifically used by property management companies, private landlords, property managers, community managers, etc., all serve different purposes, there are property management reports. Given this, recognizing the property management reports provided to property owners is important for both the management company and the relationship between the owners.

These reports on property management communicate how the property is performing, what targets to focus on for that property or portfolio, and improve that relationship by building trust between the property management company and the owner.

Revenue and Expense Statement

In a simple way, an income and expense report show the income flow to the property and the payment by category of expenses from that income. The principal elements of a property owner's income and expense statement show:

- Category income
- Complete Earnings
- Spending by group
- Overall Expenses
- Complete line item, minus expenses

Owner disbursements (also known as an owner draw) are excluded as an cost because this account is from a land or lease viewpoint — so such funds are no longer accessible to the company to be used as profits.

Monitoring the financial performance of properties and examining the financial statements is one of the most important tasks for property managers. The financial performance of buildings should be reviewed monthly by the asset manager, property management director, regional manager, and property manager.

The Declaration of Profit and Loss, also known as the Income Statement, is one of the most important of all financial documents when analyzing financial documents. It tells you if the income is enough to pay off all the expenses.

Revenue: This covers both residential and commercial rental revenue, this from washing and sales, parking fees, lease fees such as maintenance, fines, missing keys.

Collection rate: One of the key factors driving a higher stream of rental income is collection rate. The collection rate in a typical residential property between 95 per cent and 98 per cent is considered acceptable. Eventually any uncollected rent will be written off and become one of the operating expenses.

Vacancies and Concessions – in some cases, you may provide a concession to motivate future residents to move in sooner to minimize losses from building vacancies. This strategy is commonly used in high turnover-intensive economic downturn or rental housing market.

Income and expenses in Property Management

Returns

Property management companies have several revenue sources which feed their income statement 's top line. Any of those sources of income can have rules and regulations, depending on where you are based. Late fees, for example, are heavily regulated: when or how they should be paid, how they should be handled, who holds them and how much they should be.

Expenses

It turns out that there are many ways of spending money on property management companies too! You should be vigilant in keeping your "net income" (revenue minus expenses) up to speed. Monthly looking at this figure makes for good fiscal hygiene. Another fundamentally sound practice is to keep on thinking about growing your customer base. Even if you have a rock-solid customer base, you 're still likely to lose a customer every now and then. That can happen entirely outside of your control for reasons. The real estate market, for example, could get stronger, and a landlord might want to sell his rental property. Like fewer clients, nothing hurts the top line of an income statement; thus, hedge against that outcome by implementing consistent growth strategies.

Categories of Expenses

Administrative expenses

- Marketing & Advertising
- Wages and benefits
- Taxes on salaries
- Office deliveries
- Accountability programs
- Litigation services
- Telephone Service
- Informatics services
- Insurance Coverage
- Employee compensation.
- *Utility Expenditures*
- Electro power
- Gas-Gas
- Clean water
- Drain water
- *Maintenance and Repair*
- Janitorial supplies
- Trash
- Landscape
- Supplies repair
- Repair contracts including plumbing, electrical, fire alarm monitoring, inspection of fire sprinklers, repair of boilers

Other expenses may include;

Admin fees: property management firms and landlords may charge admin fees to cover NSF inspections, late rent, insurance lapses, application fees, lost key fees, early termination of the lease, rent violation fees and other administrative fees.

Parking / Garage: Through charging for parking or garage space, multifamily buildings will add to their revenue.

Laundry: If your property units do not include a washer and dryer, you are probably offering the building laundry facilities. The average per charge is typically around $5 to $8 (for both washing and drying). That, even with the cost of machine repairs, can add up to considerable income. And, your tenants needn't hoof it to the local laundromat.

Storage: Despite the push to hold just what brings you joy; the truth of the matter is this: people have things. All they need to store is stuff. It doesn't always fit stylishly into their rental unit whether it's holiday decorations or children's bikes. Charging for extra storage is a surefire way to generate revenue.

Pet Rent: Animals may be part of the family, but not every real estate manager needs them. If you allow pets in your rental properties, an additional rent and security deposits will be one of the benefits. Although not all animals are going to cause issues in a home, smart property maintenance firms recognize that not all pet owners are vigilant in ensuring their position remains safe from any harm done by Fido or Fluffy. An extra $20 or $50 pet rent per month or a security deposit will mitigate any possible harm.

Energy / Cable / Insurance: Energy and cable contracts drive your real estate profits. Landlords and property firms can also receive passive ancillary income through the selling of property insurance through their rental portal.

Trash Valet: This service provides for valets to collect waste and recyclables from the doorstep of each tenant and take them to dumpsters on-site.

This is what an expense report sheet looks like.

Type	Q3/2017	Q4/2017	Q1/2018	Q2/2018	Total
Income					
Operating					
Rent Income					
Total Income from Operating	$6,000.00	$6,000.00	$6,000.00	$2,000.00	$20,000.00
Financial					
Rent Income					
Total Income from Financial	$6,000.00	$6,000.00	$6,000.00	$2,000.00	$20,000.00
Total Income	$12,000.00	$12,000.00	$12,000.00	$4,000.00	$40,000.00
Expense					
Operating					
Repairs					
Supplies					
Utilities					
Total Expense from Operating	$850.00	$850.00	$850.00	$850.00	$850.00
Financial					
Utilities					
Total Expense from Financial	$300.00	$380.00	$300.00	$100.00	$1,080.00
Total Expense	$300.00	$380.00	$300.00	$100.00	$1,080.00
Net Income from Operations	$1,150.00	$1,230.00	$1,150.00	$950.00	$4,480.00
Net Income	$1,150.00	$1,230.00	$1,150.00	$950.00	$4,480.00

INCOME REPORT

In this section for better understanding, we will be using a companies' report for an example as majority of these statements and reports have been exclusively explained earlier or above.

Income Statement

	Cash Basis, from Jan 1, 2018 to March 31, 2018, by Month			
Property				
259 Maison Court, Unit 301				
	Jan 2018	Feb 2018	Mar 2018	2018 Total
Income				
Rent	$2,300	$2,300	$2,300	$6,900
Late Fee		$100		$100
Parking	$300	$300	$300	$900
Storage	$50	$50	$50	$150
Other		$60		$60
Total Income	$2,650	$2,810	$2,650	$8,110
Expenses				
Appliance Repair		$535		$535
Building Services	$400			$400
Marketing/Advertising			$240	$240
				$1,175
Total Expenses	$400.00	$535	$240.00	$2,350
Net Operating Income	$2,250	$2,275	$2,210	$5,760
Net Income	$2,250	$2,275	$2,210	$6,735

Successful real estate investors and real estate managers need data. And they need organized data to provide insight, control costs and maximize real estate revenue.

Good feelings about the "bottom line" must be based on accurate data, insight on which you can rely and make good long-term decisions, and keep your property management business in the dark. And if this is in real time, it is even better.

Reports of income inform you about the health of your property management company, and the quality of return for owners / investors (reports of owners). They can also help you forecast ahead.

Reports on income give a quick yet deep insight into key financial data — revenue and expenses. When you see these data presented in charts, you gain a better appreciation of the pulse of your business and sensitivity to factors that drive sustainability for your business.

Let's not take sustainability of the business or investment for granted. Short-term wins and lucky breaks combined make for a precarious business perspective. Data tells you a lot about which properties, tenants and long-term revenue strategies actually work. Are you flying at night, or on a long haul in it?

The information on your income statement should represent your current financial position for each and every one of your operated assets.

Do CFOs take income statements to heart? You bet, that is the essence of what they're doing. They watch it as a hawk for cash flow, earnings, future crises, income loss, and how company revenue is receptive to events all year long. It can help you become aware of the key variables in your revenue flow.

Things that should be included in the declaration of income / expense

Office and maintenance supplies, utilities, bookkeeping, cleaning services, insurance, tenant screening, utility bills, mortgages and more could also be included. Revenue and expenses of course depend on the details of the property owner 's agreement with you.

There are plenty of other financial reports that property managers should provide to owners including the owners report, but the income and expense statement is the most important to investors and owners.

Using the data visualization features of your property management software, you can review the performance of your entirely managed properties.

The best tools for land management

In addition to streamlining tenant and owner communications and automating day-to-day workload, the best software for property management helps you report the value you give to property owners. Documents express their investment's health and potential.

CHAPTER 7
ILLEGAL ACTIVITIES

A crime is a wrongdoing punishable by a state or other authority. The term crime does not have any simple and universally accepted definition in modern criminal law, though for certain purposes statutory definitions have been provided. The most popular view is that crime is a category created by law; in other words, something is a crime if the relevant and applicable law declares it to be such. One definition proposed is that a crime or offense (or criminal offense) is an act that is harmful not only to some individual, but also to a community, society, or state ('a public

mistake'). Such acts are prohibited and are punishable by law.

Real estate deals and contacts are the line of work done by a broker while at work. He or she is dealing with clients, communicating with lawyers and real estate agents, as well as surveyors and agencies. It is his or her responsibility to ensure proper completion of the transactions and sales. There are some cases, however, where the broker can commit fraud either deliberately or without his or her knowledge. Because of these illegal activities, some may lose their employment while others need training to know what constitutes fraud and what is merely bending the laws.

Misinterpretation in sales

The primary concern regarding broker fraud is the misrepresentation of some key factors of a sale. Some might give false details about themselves, such as credentials, background and history of work. These and other fraudulent activities are most prevalent in real estate transactions. Brokerage fraud occurs when the entire company or agency undertakes similar fraudulent actions as a single broker. Unfortunately, the company or single professional may commit the actions repeatedly without knowing this is a crime until someone contacts the authorities or explains the matter to another professional. Some may experience an attorney hired by the firm offering training classes to recognize fraud.

Examples of Broker Fraud

Scams form a big part of broker fraud. Through the scam the broker can engage in illegal activity and continue to charge a person for various problems. He or she may also provide a foreclosure listing in the full disclosure of various details, or may not follow the requirements. He or she may misrepresent a property by age, background, size, and defects. He or she may even use a false license or provide fake credentials for the buyer or seller to continue his or her business or scam. In certain cases, he or she can delegate the work for which he or she is liable to another person without obtaining the buyer's consent. Full disclosure is necessary along with the customer's appropriate duty of care. It is the broker 's task to provide all the information, remain honest and provide the buyer or seller with the data about situations. In real estate matters, the client places confidence in a broker and important is the duty to perform the proper function. If the broker breaches the duty of performing his or her duties, he or she could face a lawsuit against him or her for the breach. Then, for some time, he or she may face a negative impact on his or her career, or land in prison or jail.

Damage and effects to the victims

In broker fraud the primary concern is the damage to the customer. If he or she is suffering from a scam initiated by the broker, he or she may need to hire an attorney and litigate against the pro. The worst the crime, the more compensation the client would need. If the property has several debts or extra payments added to it, the new buyer may either have to reverse any of these procedures or compel the broker to pay back the money by means of a court order. It is usually less likely to collect evidence when the broker cannot cover his or her tracks. Other consequences could result in different types of compensation being given to the client to include punitive damages if the judge determines that the broker has to face additional punishment. The recovery of damages is a victim's right. The broker may face monetary fines for the activity. Depending on what the broker has engaged in with the client or a financial institution, criminal charges are possible. A broker 's reputation and professional life may end if he or she is caught engaging in real estate brokering fraud. Then, perhaps he or she needs to find another line of work.

What is Fraud in Real Estate?

The crime of real estate fraud occurs when one party to a real estate transaction misrepresents the other party with relevant information. The other party then acts, to their financial detriment, on the false information. In many contexts, real estate fraud occurs, including the closing (sale or purchase) of a piece of real estate, and the application for or approval of a mortgage. Fraud in real estate can be punishable by jail time and/or monetary fines.

What is Real Estate Fraud 's Elements?

To prove fraud against immovable property, the prosecutor must demonstrate the following:

- One party is making a mistake, or omitting a (relevant) fact to another;
- The party which makes the mistake or omission intends to commit fraud;
- In making a decision, the other party relies on the misstatement, such as a decision to accept a loan or buy a home; and
- The other party is incurring financial loss as a result of that reliance.

You have to show a loss. Depending on the circumstances, even the lost chance to buy a home could be considered a financial loss.

Property Law.

Property law is the area of law which governs the various forms of real estate (land) and personal property ownership. Property refers to legally protected claims to resources including intellectual property, such as land and personal property. Property can be exchanged through contract law and if property is infringed one could sue for protecting it under tort law. Property principle, theory, or philosophy underlies all property law. In some jurisdictions, the monarch historically owned all the property and devolved it through feudal land tenure or other feudal loyalty and fealty systems.

Property Crime.

Property crime is a category of crime, typically involving private property, including, but not limited to, crime, burglary, larceny, theft, theft of motor vehicles, arson, shoplifting and vandalism. Crime at property is a crime to get money, property, or some other benefit. In cases like robbery or extortion, this may involve force, or the threat of force. Since these crimes are committed to enrich the perpetrator, they are considered crimes against property. Crimes against property are classified into two groups: property lost, and property stolen. When property is destroyed it might be called incendiary or vandalism. Robbery or embezzlement are examples of the act of stealing property.

Property crimes include various specific offenses related to theft or loss of property by another person. They can range from lower-level crimes including shoplifting or vandalism to high-level felonies like armed robbery and arson attacks. Some of these crimes do not require the offender to make off with stolen goods or even harm a victim-such as a burglary, which requires only unlawful entry with the intent to commit a crime. Others demand that money or properties be genuinely taken away. Some involve a victim present at the time of the crime, such as robbery. Most property crimes have a variety of degrees based on factors including the amount taken and the use of force or guns in burglary related cases, and real or possible bodily harm in property destruction crimes such as arson.

Theft

Theft is the act of intentionally depriving others of the property they own. Many states use the word to describe a wide variety of crimes against land, such as larceny and robbery. Theft is a property crime involving taking another person's property or services, without the consent of the other person. Theft may be achieved without knowledge of the other person, by tricking the other person, or by threatening or harassing them. The items that have been taken may be tangible, such as vehicles, clothes, tools, etc. Theft may also be of services such as making a homeowner pay someone in the winter to snow blow their driveway and the individual never complete the job. Theft is normally punishable by jail time in most jurisdictions.

larceny

One commits larceny by taking something of value without consent and with the intention of permanently depriving the object's rightful proprietor. Instead of larceny most states use the term theft.

Burglary

Burglary is the unlawful entry into a closed home or other structure, often by force or coercion, with the intention of stealing property from another, or committing some other crime. Burglary is a property crime involving breaking and entering a commercial establishment or a home for the intent of committing some sort of crime inside, like stealing. Up to 50 per cent of burglaries are not reported, and this is due to its incredibly low solvency rate. In the late summer, burglaries tend to occur most and are most likely to occur during the day, when the odds are good that no one will be home. In most states, Burglary is punishable by a prison sanction if a person is convicted of the crime.

Neighborhood watch is a crime prevention initiative developed by members of the community to deter crime in their neighborhoods. Neighborhood Watch programs with the right organization and commitment can be very successful in preventing or solving the burglaries.

An example of a burglary would be if a person broke a window and climbed it through. The person then stole a couple of lamps and a television, left the window behind, and ran away with the items.

Robbery

One commits robbery by using force or the threat of force, such as pointing a gun at a bank teller and demanding cash, to take money or property from another. A person commits robbery when using violence or the threat of violence to take possessions or money from someone. Robberies happen at different locations, including banks and convenience stores. A robber may point a gun at a bank teller or cashier and demand money. It is also the taking of property by force or threats from an immediate possession of an individual. A person who has been entrusted with the property but then unlawfully takes it is guilty of Embezzlement. Extortion occurs when one person obtains money, property or services from another person through violence, intimidation or physical harm threats. Threats may include damage to the body, properties and credibility of the victim. Blackmail is a crime of threatening to expose to the media, a family member or associates significantly truthful information about an individual unless a victim's demand is met. Theft of motor vehicles includes auto stealing.

Shoplifting

Shoplifting is the theft or concealment of a retail establishment's merchandise without the intention of paying for it, such as putting items in one's pocket and going out of a store. It is shoplifting when someone steals or conceals goods from a store. This usually happens when someone in a bag or pocket hides a piece of merchandise and walks out of the store. At almost any retail establishment, including grocery stores, department stores, and clothing stores, a thief will shoplift.

Arson

Arson is the deliberate burning of virtually every form of structure, building or forest property, with more extreme degrees recognized when it causes bodily harm, or includes an occupied building or an attempt to defraud insurers. Arson is one of the most serious types of property offences. When a person burns some land or building, he or she commits arson. Charges may be more serious if investors were to be defrauded or someone injured.

Misdemeanor

Vandalism happens when an person, without their permission, damages, defaults or otherwise degrades someone else's property; sometimes it is called criminal harm, malicious trespass or malicious mischief. The crime of vandalism occurs when a individual defaults or damages property without permission. Graffiti, breaking windows, throwing eggs and slashing tires are examples of vandalism. Other vandalism terms include criminal harm, malicious mischief, and malicious trespass.

Vandalism and Misdemeanor Insurance.

Vandalism and malicious mischief insurance are a type of insurance coverage which protects against vandal-related losses. Some common commercial and homeowner plans include theft and malicious mischief protection. This is important for property, such as with churches and schools, which are not occupied during well-known periods of the day. Because these buildings are unoccupied, vandals are targets because the vandals know there is a reduced chance of being captured. Such coverage usually entails a higher penalty for property considered to be unoccupied due to the danger and severity of damage (such as churches and schools) at those hours of the day. Vandalism and mishap are described as intentional injury or property destruction. In the event that the legislation needs additional support for this form of reporting, vandalism and malicious damage may be written as a support of existing regulations, such as standard fire legislation.

Vandalism is damage to the property of another, just for the sake of causing harm. Malicious mischief is similar but it may not have been intended to inflict harm. Some stuff goes straddle the track, depending on the result, like egging a house. Vandalism is one of the most common crimes relating to property.

The danger of vandalism or malicious mischief encompasses damage to parts of the premises you are responsible for, as well as personal property. If someone slashes your bike's tires at the premises, that's vandalism. That's vandalism if someone thinks your music is too loud and sneaks into your home to destroy your stereo. Both damages will definitely be compensated if they met the deductible.

What is the most common type of vandalism which results in claims for insurance? Furious exes. Exes, which were often fueled by alcohol, were known to cause property damage and destruction as revenge. When an ex enters the home and throws it away, that's vandalism and it's normally covered up.

EVICTION

Eviction is the landlord's eviction of a tenant from his rental house. In some jurisdictions, it may also involve removing persons from premises that a mortgagee has foreclosed (often the previous owners who have defaulted on a mortgage). Depending on the jurisdiction 's laws, eviction may also be referred to as unlawful detainer, summary possession, summary dispossess, summary process, forcible detention, ejection, and repossession, among other conditions. Nonetheless, the word eviction is the most widely used in landlord-tenant communications.

Depending on the jurisdiction involved a landlord must win an eviction case or succeed in another phase of the legal process before a tenant can be expelled. It should be borne in mind that eviction, as with ejectment and certain other related terms, has precise meanings only in certain historical contexts or with respect to specific jurisdictions. There has come to be a broad variety in the meaning of these words in current practice and procedure, from jurisdiction to jurisdiction. File this easily and early in the month when an eviction is required.

For whatever reason, you may file between the fifth and tenth of the month. Once the eviction is filed, it takes 30 to 45 days to complete the process and the goal is to get the tenant to vacate amicably. The tenant will be there on occasion right up to the last moments of the eviction. The tenant must then legally remove any personal items at that time. If anything in value exceeding $500 is left behind, the management company shall have the right to legally remove the property and place it at the curbside.

Phase of the court of expulsion

Filing an eviction requires two or three visits to the office of the Magistrate. The first visit is going to cost from $40 to $50. Then it will cost between $5 and $10 for second and third visits. An eviction has a total actual cost of less than $100. The end result is the tenant leaving your property and as soon as possible finding a new tenant. A property management company will try to resolve this friendly and get the tenants out of the property they are vacating without any reason to disrespect.

During the process of eviction, tenants may request a hearing on show cause. If that happens, the process could be delayed, but not by long. It requires the landlord or property manager to attend a court hearing to provide proof to the judge as to why the expulsion is being filed. Usually this is just a formality, but it is a way to delay the process for tenants. Having the hearing is their right.

Further explained, eviction is an official legal proceeding to be followed by a property owner to have the tenant move out. When it comes to evicting a tenant there are different rules. These rules vary from state to state, and within a state, sometimes from town to city. However, there are several general concerns that land owners and real estate administrators should be mindful of when expelling a tenant.

- Notices of eviction on cause
- Notices of dispossession without cause
- Defenses which are available to tenants
- How to take out a tenant
- Reasons for strict rules on eviction

These are important issues which affect the eviction process for landlords and property managers. And while researching your particular state laws is best, having a general understanding of the rules for evicting a tenant can help you understand the laws in your state better.

Cause Notice of Eviction

A notice of eviction for cause may come in a variety of forms, but it all stems from a tenant doing something wrong or against the terms of the rent. There are usually three types of notifications of eviction for reasons: pay rent or leave notifications, cure or leave notices, and notices of unconditional quit.

Pay or withhold notices

In general, pay rent or leave notices are issued by the owner for non-payment of the rent. These written notices normally give a tenant a short period of time, as laid down by state law, in which to pay rent or otherwise be subject to an eviction lawsuit.

Cure or Delete Notices

Cure or quit notices are generally sent out when a renter is doing something wrong or breaching a term of the lease agreement. These notices generally provide a tenant a short amount of time in which to cure the defect or otherwise face eviction, like a pay rent or quit notice.

ENFORCEMENT

Enforcement is the method of ensuring that legislation, regulations, guidelines, expectations and social norms are followed. Governments or other bodies of authority attempt to implement policies successfully by enforcing legislation and regulations. Law applies to the implementation of a statute or rule, or execution of an executive or judicial order.

Eviction Orders: How to enforce them.

Although a landlord alone is unable to force a tenant to move out, the Landlord and Tenant Board (LTB) may issue an Eviction Order requiring the tenant to vacate the unit.

But the directive is not implemented by the LTB. The only person capable of executing the order is an enforcement officer, known as the "Sheriff" When the landlord receives an Eviction Notice from the LTB, a copy must be brought to the Sheriff's office and obtained a document known as a Writ of Possession.

What are the execution steps?

The Sheriff shall send the tenant a written notice indicating the intention of the Sheriff to enforce the Writ of Possession. This notice is often taped at the rental unit door, and will specify the date and time of the expulsion. The Sheriff will escort the tenant out of the unit if the tenant does not vacate the premises by that date and time. Even permitting the landlord to change the locks into the building. Generally, it is allowed to vacate the premises for one week, but less time can be given if the reason for the eviction includes criminal activities or business taking place on site.

What about belongings?

If a tenant moves out of the premises following a termination notice, termination agreement, or if employment in the case of superintendents is terminated, the landlord may sell, retain, or dispose of any remaining property on the premises.

However, if a tenant moves out following an Eviction Order, the landlord must make available the tenant's belongings for 72 hours after the expulsion. The properties must be kept at or near the rental unit, and accessible daily from 8AM to 8PM. If the property is not made available, the tenant can apply to the LTB for reimbursement for the property that they lost.

In some cases a tenant who has left the unit and has not returned may be considered abandoning the unit. The landlord can get an order from the LTB which declared the unit abandoned. The landlord can then sell, retain, or dispose of any property left in the unit 30 days after issuance of the notification. Alternatively, the landlord might give the tenant notice that they will disposal of any property in the unit. The landlord may sell, keep, or dispose of any property that is still in the unit 30 days from the date the notice was issued. In this case, the occupant must pay for the storage fees paid by the landlord before the property was released if belongings are collected during this 30-day period.

BUDGETING

A budget is a defined period of a Financial Plan, often one year. It may also include planned volumes of sales and revenues, quantities of resources, costs and expenses, assets, liabilities, and cash flows. Companies, governments, families, and other groups use it in measurable terms to communicate strategic plans for activities or events. A budget is the sum of money allocated for a specific purpose and a summary of the intended expenditure along with proposals on how to meet it. It may include a budget surplus, providing money for future use or a deficit in which expenditures exceed revenue.

Capital budgeting is the process which a company undertakes to assess potential major projects or investments. Examples of projects that would require capital budgeting before they are approved or rejected are the construction of a new plant or a big investment in an outside venture.

As part of capital budgeting, a firm could evaluate the lifetime cash inflows and outflows of a prospective project to determine whether the potential returns that would be generated meet a sufficient target benchmark. The process is also known as assessment of investments.

Ideally, companies would pursue any and all of the projects and opportunities that would increase shareholder value. However, since the amount of capital available to any business for new projects is limited, management is using capital budgeting techniques to determine which projects will yield the best return over an applicable period of time.

How do you properly budget for a property?

Also if time consuming, the budget is the roadmap that will tell you your property's course, and how much cash you can expect to earn monthly. If done correctly – it will also tell you how much rent your tenants will pay you ...... both basic rent and running costs. Occasionally, tenants contact us and say how pleased they are with the building so we don't have to bring any funds to repair or maintain the building. Other tenants will offer to care for certain maintenance items such as HVAC themselves.

Which landlords need to understand that while this approach will definitely reduce operating costs and keep tenants happy, the Landlord will ultimately be hurt. What can happen is that a property is not maintained pro-actively and then the tenant leaves at the end of their lease. The landlord now has a property in his hands that they are unable to lease because it is in poor shape. They are suffering from the vacancy, and are also required to inject capital to match the property.

This would not be the case if the property had been retained all along.

For Commercial Properties – The tenants pay for the costs of running the building if you have a net Lease. At the same time – landlords have to walk the tight rope between making sure that their properties are running well but also making sure the tenants can still afford to pay the operating costs. Your property manager should have a budget ready for you three to four months to review before the end of your building year. If not, then you can follow them up to decide what's holding things up. For landlords with larger regional or national tenants, the updated rent notices should be submitted to them in plenty of time before the year-end so that their internal accounting departments and you are not in a position to keep. This way the property owner gets the rent on time.

The property manager will associate the costs with other competing buildings on an item by item basis. There are other tools for comparison and you will be able to consult the property manager on this.

Don't forget the One Time and Ongoing Costs bill. Be sure to account for both one-time and on-going expenses when you build your budget. Those recurring costs include items such as annual property assessments and repairs according to Property Ware. One-time costs may include the cost of making a property suitable after an existing landlord moves out or works with a big problem like a broken pipe. Property Ware also advises you to add a contingency fund for these unforeseen big expenses.

Do your research. Multifamily Executive says you should collect all relevant historical information, including current rents, current occupancy, 12-month trailing financial reports, salary information, and increases in utility prices, before entering numbers. Look up contracts for stuff like lawn care, ads, software, copiers, and the like; you should have a handle on things that don't alter over the year.

Determine any categories applicable to the new budget. Multifamily executive says you get to negotiate the budget together with your staff. What should be changed? What categories to add or delete? Installing electronic package lockers, for example, can you boost your facilities offerings? If you are looking to improve resident relationships and provide a premium living environment then you need to budget appropriately for amenities such as parcel lockers, smart homes, pet facilities on-site and more.

Go with your accounting electronically. Property Management Insider notes that an integrated web-based accounting system is essential to managing the budget, as it bundles all functions into one work solution. Receipts can be checked, expenditures posted and deposits made with just a few clicks. Plus, eco-friendly digital accounting solution. With a few simple practices, property management firms can stay atop the money that flows in and out of their investments and help build a healthier sector.

Set Aside Marketing and Advertising Budget. The Balance Small Business notes that word of mouth will bring in new tenants but successful business competition includes a marketing campaign and a budget for ads. Don't forget to include budget for daily ads in media that have proven track record in tenant generation. The advertisement and promotion budget would also cover the cost of keeping the listings online. It is also prudent to budge for increased marketing as vacancy rates grow. Often vital to the budget plan is to organize increased ads to announce redesign or upgrades.

MAINTENANCE

The technical meaning of maintenance includes functional checks, servicing [disambiguation required], repairing or replacing necessary devices, equipment, machinery, building infrastructure, and supporting utilities in industrial, business, governmental, and residential installations. Over time, this has come to include multiple wordings describing different cost-effective practices for keeping equipment operational; these activities occur either before or after a failure.

Property maintenance relates to the care of a residence, apartment, rental property or building and may be a business activity by a property maintenance company, a company employee who owns a home, apartment or self-storage pastime, such as regular housekeeping or cleaning. Additionally, facility management (or facility management or FM) is a professional management discipline that focuses on delivering support services efficiently and effectively to the organizations it serves. The International Organization for Standardization (ISO) defines facility management as the "organizational function that integrates people, places, processes and technology in the built environment with the aim of improving people's quality of life and core business productivity in conjunction with the auxiliary as well as the support services.

Facilities Maintenance and Rental Property Repairs

A rental property will not enjoy long-term tenant retention and decent return on investment unless properly maintained. This relates to:

- Maintenance is preventive and continuous;
- Fixed problems or malfunctions; and
- Building and remodeling

The role and responsibilities of a Manager of Rental Property

The property manager maintains real estate rentals through advertising and filling vacancies; negotiate and enforce leases; maintain and secure premises.

A property manager is a third party hired to manage the day-to-day operations of an investment in real estate. They are able to handle all types of property, from single family homes to large complexes. Responsibilities can be quite broad, including maintaining property rentals by filling out vacancies, negotiating and enforcing leases, setting and collecting rent, screening prospective tenants, handling complaints, keeping a precise budget, and maintaining and securing premises. In between the tenant and you, the owner, the property manager is. They are the "first line of protection" and they are there to protect you, to manage all problems so effectively that in the middle of the night, irate tenants or service providers don't call you.

Some of the unique obligations regarding facilities and physical maintenance and repairs can include:

- Investigating and resolving complaints by tenants; inspecting vacant units and completing repairs; planning renovations; contracting with special maintenance services such as carpentry, plumbing, electricity, landscaping and snow removal
- Supervising reparations.
- Establishing and enforcing policies and procedures for precaution; responding to emergencies;

Outstanding property managers are diligent and oriented on information.

Ongoing and preventive maintenance

Preventive and ongoing maintenance of rental properties requires a thorough knowledge of the property, its maintenance needs, staffing required to carry out the tasks (or contracting with service professionals) and budgeting to carry them out. The real estate manager has to balance the routine and preventive maintenance costs with the benefits and desired outcomes. Line items on a routine maintenance list for a property manager could include:

- Cleaning common areas;
- Conservation of the countryside;
- Heating and air conditioning systems regular service;
- Periodic plumbing and electrical object inspection;
- Wood, roofing & other building components properly maintained.

Repairs and corrective measures

When things break or fail to function as intended, repairs and corrective actions are required. Sometimes repairing is of an emergency nature, such as a winter heating malfunction, while at other times these repairs can be scheduled and effectively done in groups. It is the property manager's responsibility to know the difference, and to serve the tenants' needs while balancing costs. It's also important to be careful of small issues before they become big ones.

Construction and remanufacturing

Construction and remodeling are part of the maintenance of the facilities and buildings. The structure may need to be remodeled or constructed:

- For a commercial Tenant 's special business requirements;
- To correct structural obsolescence; or
- To fit in with a tenant's special physical needs.

A real estate manager can be highly skilled in all other management functions, but if they drop the ball when it comes to facility maintenance, the property will experience condition degradation, tenant loss, and declining rents.

RENTAL PROPERTY MANAGEMENT BODIES

Having learned the principles and guidelines of real properties, how to invest how to go about it, after being exposed to a knowledge filled structure of rental properties. If you feel you want to go into it, here are some good recommended organizations you can look up online and get more precise knowledge about their dealings.

BOMA International

BUILDING OWNERS & MANAGERS ASSOCIATION

What it is: BOMA was founded in 1907, and is a professional real estate professional organization. In states across the US, there are local BOMA associations, as well as multiple international affiliates. The BOMA mission is to "through advocacy, influence, and knowledge advance a vibrant commercial real estate industry."

Membership details: The membership base of BOMA consists of over 16,500 professionals in commercial real estate, including building owners, managers, developers, leasing professionals, asset managers and more. BOMA provides professional development services to meet the educational needs of members, and protects the rights of members through legislative lobbying activities. Advantages for membership include access to industry benchmark research and discounts on industry publications, seminars and programs.

Events: Association events include the BOMA International Conference & Expo, on-demand webinars for continuing credits for professional development, and tracks for specialty training. Check out the events calendar on BOMA.

How to join: Find a BOMA association for dues and more information in your area.

IREM

INSTITUTE OF REAL ESTATE MANAGEMENT

What it is: IREM ® is an international community of residential and commercial real estate managers dedicated to promoting ethical business practices, maximizing the value of real estate investments and promoting superior management through education and information sharing.

Membership details: IREM helps its members and those in the industry at any point of their career with preparation, professional growth, and collaboration. IREM members may earn credentials – including Certified Property Manager (CPM ®) and Accredited Residential Manager (ARM ®) – that are designed to advance their careers by demonstrating commitment to best practices in property management. Members often enjoy reduced or free rates for all IREM products and services.

Events: IREM hosts multiple events throughout the year for regional, national, and global education and networking. Visit the Events page of IREM.

How to join: Learn more about the four types of IREM memberships to choose which one suits your needs.

NAA IRO

NATIONAL APARTMENT ASSOCIATION INDEPENDENT RENTAL OWNERS

What it is: NAA is a leading voice in the rental housing market, representing more than 75,000-member firms. NAA's IRO system is geared explicitly to individuals who own or operate the rental property. Like many users of Yardi Breeze, these are often owners with smaller portfolios, who have invested their own money in the property and are actively involved in management.

Details of membership: NAA members have access to exclusive education and training, discounts and sector publications. As an IRO member your member services include your market-specific webinars, designations and resources. The topics range from concerns about fair housing and hiring to bed bugs and rent increases.

Events: See the upcoming schedule of NAA meetings, conferences, and exhibitions, which is held annually in the summer, includes specific IRO programming.

How to join: Find your local NAA affiliate and get in touch or email membership@naahq.org

NARPM

NATIONAL ASSOCIATION OF RESIDENTIAL PROPERTY MANAGERS

What it is: NARPM is a professional residential real estate professional's association as its name suggests. Founded in 1988, NARPM provides the residential property management industry with a permanent trade organization and currently represents more than 5,200 members, comprising real estate agents, brokers, managers and their staff.

Membership details: Why you should be a member of the NARPM? Members of NARPM enjoy a host of membership benefits, such as educational opportunities, mentoring and discount programs. Members may earn nationally recognized roles, from management and maintenance to bookkeeping and support. Additionally, local chapters are hosting smaller state-level events to make it easier to engage, network, and access resources from associations.

Events: NARPM conferences incorporate organized speakers, educational sessions, and networking events to promote your professional development. One of the most important conventions and vendor expos for property managers is the annual NARPM convention & trade show.

How to join: Submit your NARPM membership application online.

Source: https://www.yardibreeze.com/blog/2018/11/4-property-management-associations/

CPSIA information can be obtained
at www.ICGtesting.com
Printed in the USA
LVHW042256081020
668387LV00017B/2745